Marc E. Vargo, MS

Acts of Disclosure
The Coming-Out Process of Contemporary Gay Men

Pre-publication
REVIEWS,
COMMENTARIES,
EVALUATIONS . . .

"**A**s a researcher, I am favorably impressed by the blending of research findings with material obtained from a diversity of sources that include the descriptive literature, clinical literature, popular media, and the author's apparently astute observational abilities.

I am pleased by the sensitivity of Mr. Vargo to the feelings and concerns of heterosexual persons. Upset family members are not invariably characterized as cruel bigots but as vulnerable persons who can be deeply hurt by the announcements and decisions of the gay man who is coming out. Vargo describes the stages of adjustment that parents and wives go through in addition to the stages the gay man experiences.

This book would be an excellent one for gay men who are coming out or considering such. I believe, however, that *Acts of Disclosure* is equally informative for heterosexual persons who want to better understand the experiences of their gay friends, relatives, neighbors, and co-workers. It is clearly written and is sufficiently free of jargon for laypersons to appreciate it. It is also sophisticated enough to command the respect of professional persons such as educators, psychologists, social workers, doctors, nurses, and attorneys. My overall rating of the book is outstanding."

Donald I. Templer, PhD
Professor of Psychology,
California School of Professional
Psychology, Fresno

The Harrington Park Press
An Imprint of The Haworth Press, Inc.

Acts of Disclosure
The Coming-Out Process
of Contemporary Gay Men

HAWORTH Gay & Lesbian Studies
John P. De Cecco, PhD
Editor in Chief

Acts of Disclosure
The Coming-Out Process of Contemporary Gay Men

Marc E. Vargo, MS

The Harrington Park Press
An Imprint of The Haworth Press, Inc.
New York • London

Published by

The Harrington Park Press, an imprint of The Haworth Press, Inc., 10 Alice Street, Binghamton, NY 13904-1580

Note: Except when otherwise noted, names and other personal information that might identify those whose experiences are discussed herein have been modified to preserve their privacy. Also, in certain cases, examples are based on composites of individuals.

Material has been reprinted with permission from the following sources:

Robert L. Barret and Bryan E. Robinson, *Gay Fathers*. Copyright © 1990 Jossey-Bass Inc., Publishers. First published by Lexington Books. All rights reserved.

R. Troiden, "Becoming homosexual: A model of gay identity acquisition," *Psychiatry: Interpersonal and Biological Process*, Vol. 42. Copyright © 1979 by The Guilford Press.

F. Bozett, "Gay fathers: Evolution of gay-father identity," *American Journal of Orthopsychiatry*, Vol. 51(3). Copyright © 1981 by the *American Journal of Orthopsychiatry.*

Griffin, Carolyn Welch, Marion J. Wirth, and Arthur G. Wirth, *Beyond Acceptance: Parents of Lesbians and Gays Talk About Their Experience.* Copyright © 1996 by Carolyn Welch Griffin, Marian J. Wirth, and Arthur G. Wirth. Published by St. Martin's Press Incorporated.

Zeeland, Steve, *Barrack Buddies and Soldier Lovers.* Copyright © 1993, and Volumes 14, 18(1/2), 22, and 22(3) of the *Journal of Homosexuality.* Published by The Haworth Press.

Cover design by Monica Seifert.

The Library of Congress has cataloged the hardcover version of this book as

Vargo, Marc.
    Acts of disclosure : the coming-out process of contemporary gay men / Marc E. Vargo.
       p.   cm.
    Includes bibliographical references and index.
    ISBN 0-7890-0236-1 (alk. paper)
    1. Coming out (Sexual orientation)—United States. 2. Gay men—United States—Psychology. 3. Gay men—United States—Family relationships. 4. Gay men—Employment—United States. I. Title.
HQ76.3.U5V37 1998
305.38'9664—dc21

                                                      97-13389
                                                        CIP

ISBN 1-56023-912-3 (pbk.)

To Michael Walker, with love

ABOUT THE AUTHOR

Marc E. Vargo, MS, is a staff member in the Department of Psychology at Hammond Developmental Center in Hammond, Louisiana, where he works with impaired individuals and serves as Chairperson of the Institutional Review Board. An activist in the gay community of New Orleans, he has contributed his services to the New Orleans AIDS Task Force, a nonprofit AIDS service organization, since 1987. As an HIV Counselor with the Task Force, he has served as Co-Chairperson of its HIV Testing and Counseling Program and has facilitated several support groups for gay men who are HIV-positive. In 1992, he wrote a book titled *The HIV Test: What You Need to Know to Make an Informed Decision,* which was published and distributed in English-speaking nations by Simon & Schuster (PocketBooks Division) and licensed and translated into Japanese by the DHC Corporation, Tokyo. The author of several journal articles on topics related primarily to anxiety, his work has appeared in *Cortex,* the *British Journal of Medical Psychology,* the *Journal of the American Academy of Behavioral Medicine,* and the *Journal of Clinical Psychology.*

CONTENTS

Foreword

To say that my decision to acknowledge publicly that I am gay was the right decision for me to have made is an example of something people rarely see: a politician engaging in a gross understatement of the facts.

Acknowledging publicly that I was gay was the second best decision I have ever made in my life, and in fact, it was the prerequisite to the best decision I ever made—that being to commit to spending my life in a domestic partnership with Herb Moses. I say that coming out was the prerequisite because it was as a consequence of my having made the decision to come out that I met Herb. He is a man of great integrity, among other assets, and he would not have been interested in a relationship of any sort with someone who was trying to live half in the closet and half out. We met when he sent me a note of congratulations on my public coming out, and he has enriched my life for the past ten years.

I had been agonizing for some time over whether to acknowledge publicly my sexual orientation. I had lived the life of a very closeted gay man, complicated by the fact that I was a politician with a very public persona. Unfortunately, it was a dishonest public persona. By the time I was in my mid-thirties, I had stopped pretending to be straight, but I was not acknowledging that I was gay. What I was was miserable.

When I got to Congress in 1981, at the age of forty-one, I thought I could prove that Abraham Lincoln was wrong, at least as regards an individual, and that I could live half slave and half free. That is, I decided I would continue to enslave myself to homophobia by failing to live as a gay man in my public life, while in fact living freely and honestly in my private life. That simply does not work. The tensions, conflicts, evasions, etc., inherent in that effort to live a double life instead caused me to make a couple of stupid mistakes in my personal life while turning up the stress level that interfered with my ability to accomplish my public goals.

By early 1987, I decided that this was a foolish way to live. And I committed myself at that point to coming out publicly. But even here I made a fundamental mistake. I assumed I would be engaging in a trade-off, in which a freedom to live my life in a sensible, rational, integrated way would produce significant personal gains, while the fact that I was acknowledging that I was gay would cause some drop in my ability to be successful in my public career. In fact, after I voluntarily announced to an inquiring reporter in May of 1987 that I was gay—having first, to be candid, told the reporter in question that I would answer the question honestly if she asked me—I found that both my public and private lives were enhanced. The private part of that is obvious. I was now free to be who I was without worrying that the real me might somehow be revealed. I met Herb and was for the first time in my life free to share my life privately and publicly with a man I loved, to participate with him as a couple in those parts of American life that are particularly open to couples, to attend congressional functions with my spouse in the same way that other members of Congress attended, and so forth.

But to my surprise, I found that my public life also benefited. Not only was there virtually no negative fallout among either the voters or my colleagues from my being honest, to some extent I reaped benefits from people who admired my honesty—graciously over-looking the previous years of dishonesty, at first explicit and then implicit. And most important, because I was happier, living an integrated life, and not spending a good deal of energy worrying about who would find out what and when, I was much better able to do my job.

The experience I had in coming out confirms a point that I think is of great importance both for those of us thinking about the personal decision and for our choices as a community in picking a political strategy. That point is that most Americans are less homophobic than they think they are supposed to be. Having grown up in a bigoted society, the average American has long thought that if he or she did not evince antihomosexual feelings, others would think less of him or her. In my experience, most people do not have such feelings, at least not to any great degree, and to the extent that they do have, they tend to dissipate when they meet people whom they know to be gay or lesbian.

To be more precise about what in fact happens, people's antihomosexual feelings dissipate not when they meet gay men and lesbians for the first time, but when people they have known for a long time as relatives, co-workers, friends, colleagues, etc., turn out to be gay or lesbian. As Herb has said, the experience of prejudice has led many gay men and lesbians to think too little of our straight friends and relatives. We tend to assume that they will remain unshakably bigoted when we tell them the truth about ourselves. And in fact our experience has more often than not been the opposite.

As a politician committed to fighting against antigay and lesbian prejudice, I believe deeply that nothing helps our cause more than having people come out to those who love, admire, and respect them. If in fact that coming-out process generally led to harm for the individuals, I would be conflicted. I would find myself having to choose between advising people to do something I thought was good for the cause in general, and telling them to protect themselves and avoid a coming-out process that would harm them.

Fortunately, in the real world, such a dilemma rarely exists. Coming out is good for the polity and it is good for the person. Never have I personally worried so much about a decision that turned out to have been so obviously the right one to make. And to others contemplating coming out, I can only say, as one who took the plunge ten years ago, come on in—the water is fine.

Barney Frank, U.S. House of Representatives;
Author, *Speaking Frankly: What's Wrong
with the Democratic Party and How to Fix It*

The purpose of life is undoubtedly to know oneself.

—*Mahatma Gandhi, 1932*

Introduction

A flashpoint in gay history: On a hot summer night in 1969, at the height of the civil rights and antiwar movements, nine New York City policemen raid the Stonewall Inn, a gay bar, claiming it lacks a license to sell liquor. In truth, the raid is but one of several tactics used routinely by the police to harass and intimidate the gay citizenry, maneuvers designed to ensure that this segment of the population remains vulnerable and subdued. But on this particular evening, the patrons of the bar, largely drag queens indignant at being bullied relentlessly by the cops, refuse to submit to the injustice and instead retaliate *en masse* in the streets. Within hours, their numbers swelling into the hundreds, they hurl bricks and bottles until the officers take cover inside the bar. Then, out of the mayhem comes an enraged demonstrator who tries to set fire to the establishment.

This incident has come to be known, of course, as the Stonewall Uprising, the moment when the American gay population kicked down the closet door. It was the fountainhead of a new revolution, the dawn of the gay liberation movement. But it was also a divisive moment within the gay world itself, revealing a difference in perspective that persists, to some extent, even today. It exposed the chasm that exists between those who hold that a person's sexual disposition is a private matter and, as such, should be shielded from public view and those who argue that a homosexual orientation is a fundamental personal characteristic and, for this reason, should be expressed openly.

To be sure, before the Stonewall riots, millions of gay men and women were compelled by circumstances to lead shadowy lives. They had little choice. In fact, due to the hostile climate of the times, not only did they scrupulously hide their own sexual orientations, but usually went to considerable lengths to protect the identities of other gay people as well. Known as guarding "The Secret," the safekeeping of all homosexual citizens' privacy was foremost among the gay community's values, a defining feature and a survival mechanism.

But times have changed. In the years since Stonewall, this conventional code of secrecy has come under fire, with a substantial share of the gay population now finding it both outmoded and problematic. Many believe that the silence it produces contributes heavily to society's ignorance about gay issues and gay lives, feeding its fears and fostering its intolerance. They favor, as an alternative, heightened visibility as a principal strategy for gaining recognition, believing it to be a far more effective method for eliminating antigay prejudice. Enhanced visibility, they say, offers an opportunity for dialogue, an occasion to educate, and a prospect for social progress. Accordingly, within the contemporary gay movement there now exists a powerful pressure for men and women to come out, to present themselves candidly and confidently to society at large. Through such mass acts of self-revelation, it is argued that the gay citizenry may at last attain equal social and legal standing with the majority population.

Of course, beyond its purely political value, such candor may also yield several important benefits for the individual, including enhanced mental health and spiritual well-being. Whereas remaining in the closet may create or intensify existing identity problems and generate feelings of anxiety, self-loathing, guilt, and depression—a predictable result, given the time and energy that one must expend to ensure that the mask does not slip off—the act of coming out is usually accompanied, sooner or later, by feelings of enriched mental and spiritual health. It liberates a person at a profound psychological level, freeing him to move on to other aspects of life, and to do so with integrity and self-respect.

And yet, its myriad benefits notwithstanding, the coming-out process can be both arduous and continuous; novel circumstances may arise from time to time that require the person to decide, yet again, whether and how to reveal this information to others. But it is also an intriguing human experience, both for the individual who undergoes it and for the researcher who studies it. In fact, for several years now, the process has been investigated by social scientists, as well as by those in other fields of inquiry.

In the chapters that follow, the findings from the most significant studies of the coming-out process conducted during the past twenty-five years are reviewed. These studies have, until now, been confined largely to the pages of professional journals. We focus specifically on gay men, since nearly all of the coming-out research has looked at adult males exclusively—a conventional, if myopic, practice in many areas of scientific inquiry. It is for this reason that the text is written in the masculine voice. Suffice it to say, the few studies that have examined the coming-out process in women suggest that it may be somewhat different for them—not an unexpected finding, given that the social roles of the two genders are defined so differently in our society. Clearly, further research is needed if we are to understand the process of sexual self-disclosure in the lesbian population.

In terms of content, Chapter 1 begins with a brief review of the research on the biological foundations of sexual orientation and proceeds to those studies that have focused on the gay child's early development and sexual awakening during adolescence. It then follows his subsequent efforts to adjust to his same-sex disposition, including his journey through a five-stage process that culminates in the disclosure of his sexual orientation to another person.

In Chapter 2, the coming-out process is further explored as the gay person reveals his sexual orientation to his family. Here the experiences of the gay youth are examined as he comes out to his mother and father, and current research on parental reactions to the news is discussed. Included as well are studies of the experiences of gay fathers who come out to their children and gay husbands who open up to their wives.

In Chapter 3, the self-disclosure process is broadened even further to encompass the workplace, with a review of those studies that have examined the coming-out experience in four representative fields of the American workforce: elementary and secondary education, the sciences, business and industry, and the armed forces.

Finally, Chapter 4 examines the process of becoming known as gay at the public level, either by being *outed* (being exposed involuntarily as homosexual) or by intentionally declaring one's same-sex orientation in the public arena. To illustrate the relevant issues, the experiences of several public figures who have come forward as gay are recounted, renowned figures in politics, sports, and the military, including the effects that the publicity has had on their personal and professional lives.

In essence, the book covers the coming-out process from the moment of conception to the declaration at the public level that one is gay. In addition to research findings, each chapter includes recommendations and advice for both gay and straight readers, along with first-person accounts of the coming-out process by those who have gone through it; statements by gay people from all walks of life who have revealed their sexual orientations in an array of settings. The aim is to place the strictly quantitative research findings in a meaningful human context, as well as to tap into the collective wisdom of the gay population itself. To be sure, it is through the sharing of our stories that we inform and fortify one another, merging our knowledge and our strength, and in this way forge a more enlightened, more empowered gay citizenry.

Chapter 1

The Coming-Out Process

Coming out was one of the hardest things I've ever done. When you're growing up and you're told all the time about how awful gays are, and then one day it dawns on you that you are one, well, it can be tough. I know I was depressed at first. But you get over it and go on with your life, and then one day you start to feel pretty good about it all. You start to realize it's okay to be gay.... My only regret is that I didn't know earlier. I think back to all those years of not knowing or else trying to run away from it. I wish I'd known I was gay when I was a kid, so I could've had a head start dealing with it.

The man who spoke these words, a thirty-four-year-old instructor of the humanities, echoes the sentiments of many gay men. And he is right. The coming-out process might be much easier if a person were able to recognize at the beginning of his life that he is homosexual. But a man does not enter the world knowing that he is gay; like other fundamental aspects of his being, his sexuality is something he must discover for himself. And this takes time. Yet the time at which his homosexual orientation itself begins to develop is another matter. For several decades now, psychologists have claimed that a child, as a result of his relationships with his father and mother, forms an affinity for either the same sex or the opposite sex by the time he is five years old, an affinity that eventually crystallizes into an enduring sexual orientation. But today, a growing body of research is finding that a considerable share of a person's sexual disposition may be present much earlier than the childhood years; indeed, even before one is born.

THE ORIGINS OF HOMOSEXUALITY

In this regard, researchers in the biological sciences have accumulated compelling evidence in recent years suggesting that homosexuality, like heterosexuality, may be a feature that is to some degree inherited. To better understand this assertion, in this section we review the major studies that have explored the biological foundations of the same-sex orientation, with particular attention to the cognitive, neuroanatomical, and DNA research. We begin our discussion, however, by looking at recent sibling studies in this area since inheritance patterns can often be uncovered by examining brothers and sisters reared in the same or different environments.

Sibling Studies

Perhaps the most important investigation to explore sexual orientation in siblings was published in 1993 by Dean Hamer and his associates at the National Institutes of Health in Bethesda, Maryland.[1] These researchers found that a man who has a gay brother has a 13 percent chance of being gay himself, whereas a man who does not have a homosexual brother stands only a 2 percent chance—a striking statistical difference. Notable differences were also found in six additional studies, which revealed that a man having a gay identical twin has a 57 percent chance of being homosexual himself compared to a man having a gay fraternal twin, who has only a 24 percent chance.[2] And this is an important finding, since identical twins occupy the same egg *in utero* and, for this reason, share a much larger amount of genetic material than do fraternal pairs. It would appear, then, that as twins become more alike in their genetic makeup, so, too, do they become more alike in their sexual orientations. As for the role of the home environment in determining sexual disposition, because brothers, like those in the studies cited here, are reared largely under the same conditions, it is believed that the family milieu, in and of itself, cannot account for such marked statistical differences.

Regarding the source of the genetic material itself, it appears that the mother may be the one who passes it on to her son. The Hamer study found that a homosexual orientation is often associated with the mother's side of the family, while showing no clear connection to the father's side.[3] In fact, for a given homosexual man, there is an 8 percent chance that he has a gay cousin in his mother's family and a 7 percent likelihood that he has a gay uncle. Furthermore, if there are two gay brothers in the same family, thus increasing the probability of a genetic basis for their homosexuality, the odds are 13 percent that they have a gay maternal cousin and 10 percent that they have a gay maternal uncle.

To be sure, findings like these lend credence to the notion of a biological foundation for sexual orientation. Based on such figures, one researcher has estimated that up to 70 percent of a person's same-sex nature may be inherited.[4]

Cognitive Research

Other investigators have explored the workings of the brain itself to determine if measurable differences exist between gay and straight men. Cheryl McCormick and her colleagues, for instance, looked at hand preference and discovered that, compared to straight men, gay men are more likely to be left-handed or to use their right hands for some tasks and their left hands for others,[5] a difference between the two orientations that is almost certainly due to neurological factors.

Other studies have found that gay and straight men differ in their abilities on certain types of mental tasks. "On the average, gay men are worse at spatial tasks and better at verbal tasks than straight men," explains one investigator.[6] Indeed, on tests of natural spatial ability, such as a mental rotation task that requires a person to visualize an object revolving in space, homosexual men score lower than heterosexual ones[7]—a difference, like handedness, that is almost certainly the result of dissimilarities in the way in which these men's brains are constructed.

Neuroanatomical Research

Still other researchers, rather than speculating that the brains of these men may be structured differently, have sought to explore the matter in a much more definitive fashion; namely, by performing post mortem exams on the brains of gay and straight men.

The first study of this type came from Europe in 1990, where Dick Swaab of the Netherlands Institute for Brain Research reported that, while examining the brains of homosexual and heterosexual men, he discovered significant differences in the size of a structure—the suprachiasmatic nucleus—that governs body rhythms.[8] As could be expected, this was a stunning revelation since no physical differences had ever before been detected.

The following year, researcher Simon LeVay at the Salk Institute made a similar announcement. Examining the brains of forty-one gay and straight men, he found that a part of the hypothalamus, a structure involved in sexual functioning, was two to three times larger in straight men than in gay men; this discovery, according to LeVay, suggests that "gay and straight men may differ in the central neuronal mechanisms that regulate sexual behavior."[9] Statistically, the odds of such size discrepancies being due to chance are one in one thousand.[10]

Also in 1991, a University of California at Los Angeles research team led by Laura Allen and Roger Gorski discovered that a bundle of nerves connecting the two hemispheres of the brain is, on the average, 34 percent larger in gay men than in straight men.[11] Thus, like the results of the other neuroanatomical studies, these findings imply that the neurological makeup of homosexual and heterosexual men is different, presumably in such a way as to contribute to remarkably disparate affectional and sexual interests in adult life.

DNA Research

Most of the studies mentioned above were based on the notion that a gay man is programmed biologically to become gay. The sibling studies point toward this possibility, while much of the research on cognitive and neuroanatomical differences stems from the assumption that it is genetic factors that account for the dissimilar development of these men's brains. It should come as no surprise, then, that in laboratories around the world there is currently a race to find the "gay gene," the single piece of evidence that would prove beyond doubt that, at the starting point of the gay man's existence, he is placed on the path toward homosexuality.

At this time, of course, we have not located such a gene. If and when we do, however, it is unlikely that its existence will, in and of itself, account for homosexuality in all cases. Human sexual functioning may be far too complex to be caused by a single agent. In fact, most researchers believe that other factors may well be necessary to bring one's homosexual orientation to full bloom, factors that may include specific conditions or events in the childhood years or possibly later in life. Some even argue that certain men may become gay for nonbiological reasons.

Nevertheless, the search for the gay gene continues to be a crucial avenue of inquiry, since its discovery would mean that at least a portion of the same-sex disposition is almost certainly predetermined. It would also help account for many, if not all, of the neurological differences between gay and straight men found in the studies that we have just discussed.

As for the current state of our search for this entity, an investigation by Dr. Hamer and his colleagues has provided a solid starting point. In 1993, this team examined DNA in sets of gay brothers and straight brothers to determine if differences could be detected in their chromosomal makeup. And, indeed, they uncovered a remarkable difference: the homosexual brothers shared a particular chromosomal pattern 82 percent of the time, the odds of which are less than one in two hundred, while the heterosexual brothers displayed this pattern no more than would be expected by chance.[12] These results, then, strongly suggest that important chromosomal differences do exist between the two sexual dispositions.

DNA, of course, is the blueprint of what we are to become. Unlike our physical bodies, which change over the course of time—our bones soften, our brains deteriorate—DNA, by and large, does not change; at most, it may show subtle effects of aging. Consequently, by studying it at any point in an individual's lifetime, even after his death, we are able to find what existed before he was formed; that is, the code that determined, in part, who he was to become. In the case of sexual orientation, dissimilarities between the DNA of gay and straight men may mean that in certain respects these gentlemen were designed to be different *at conception*. Accordingly, Dr. Hamer concludes that, within this one genetic area, we can account for a significant degree of an individual's sexual disposition.[13] Indeed, both Drs. LeVay and Hamer concur that recent genetic research "provides the strongest evidence to date that human sexuality is influenced by heredity because it directly examines the genetic information, the DNA."[14]

Thus, the preponderance of biological research—sibling studies, cognitive research, neuroanatomical investigations, DNA analyses—suggests that a gay man's sexual orientation, like that of his straight counterpart, may be established to some degree before he is born. It implies, too, that sexual orientation is a permanent condition. Like eye color or height, it is largely a given, such that any attempt to radically alter it may violate the individual's wholeness and integrity as an organism.

Play Research

In terms of the gay child's development after birth, studies indicate that it may follow a fairly typical pattern, with the homosexual child displaying noticeable differences from the straight child sometimes as early as the first year of life, according to UCLA researcher Richard Green.[15] In a longitudinal study, Dr. Green tracked forty-four boys displaying conventionally feminine interests—the so-called "sissy-boy" syndrome—from childhood through adulthood, and discovered that two-thirds of these children became homosexual or bisexual as adults. These findings support what earlier studies have implied, namely that boys who are most apt to be homosexual as adults usually dislike rough, competitive sports, preferring instead more tranquil activities, such as reading; also, that they are inclined to play with girls, not boys,[16] dress in girls' clothing for fun, play with dolls instead of trucks, and assume the role of mother, not father, when playing house.[17] This should not be taken to mean, however, that the pursuit of feminine interests causes a male child to become gay; rather, it is presumably his homosexual orientation, which is already in place, that causes him to have such interests in the first place. Nor do the findings mean that effeminate boys invariably become gay men—25 percent of them do not—rather that marked differences in patterns of childhood interests distinguish a great many gay children from straight ones. And this insight is intriguing, given that a considerable amount of play, in most species, is biologically driven.

In this regard, LeVay, among others, has proposed that "sex-typical" play is under hormonal influence; moreover, that gay men, regardless of their degree of masculinity as adults, report having engaged in a certain amount of childhood play that was characteristic of the opposite sex.[18]

In all, then, this research into play patterns bolsters the notion that certain aspects of homosexuality may be biologically determined; that the course of the gay child's development may be designed, in part, to prepare him for a same-sex adulthood. Yet this does not mean that the boy who is destined to be homosexual knows that this is the case. The fact is, he usually does *not* know, partly because he is typically raised in a heterosexual household by parents who treat him as if he were straight, the result being that he initially thinks of himself in conventional, nongay terms. In spite of this early lack of self-awareness, however, the boy may still be drawn to other males during his early years, not realizing that he is remarkable in this respect—that compared to other boys, he is much more attuned to his own gender.

"I can remember being attracted to men as far back as age seven or eight," recalls Greg Louganis, four-time Olympic gold-medalist in his autobiography, *Breaking the Surface*.[19] "I didn't understand what it meant, but I knew what my feelings were. At that age, I just assumed that's how everyone felt."

Another youth recalled the following:

> As far back as I can remember, I always had feelings of love for other boys and men in my life. . . . It wasn't until I was nineteen years old and away at college that I first realized all the other men in the world didn't feel the same way I did.[20]

And yet, while a gay youth may feel that he is like everyone else when it comes to sexual matters, he may feel different in other, nonsexual ways. And this brings us to the first stage of the coming-out process, the stage in which the youth who is unaware that he is gay finds himself feeling unlike other boys in important respects.

STAGE 1: THE PRE-COMING-OUT YEARS

Researcher Richard Troiden of Miami University interviewed 150 gay men in New York and Minnesota about their childhoods and found that, before they reached their teens, 72 percent of them had experienced a "sense of apartness" from other people.[21] "I never felt as if I fit in," said one of the men. "I don't know why for sure. I felt different. I thought it was because I was more sensitive."[22] Yet most of the men in the study did not attribute such feelings of isolation to sexual factors. In fact, nearly all of them said that they were largely unaware of their sexual orientations during this early period in their lives.

Of course, it is possible that this sense of being different is simply a natural aspect of human development and, as such, is not necessarily limited to gay youth. As researcher Troiden points out, it may be that straight men, were they to be asked, would recall that they, too, felt alienated during their adolescent years. Surely most heterosexual youths feel awkward, atypical, and alone at times, although perhaps not as frequently or intensely as homosexual youths. But one thing is certain: for a considerable number of gay men, there exists a need to look back to their childhoods for evidence that they were meant to be gay—that their homosexuality was destined to happen—with such proof most often being found in their early feelings of being unlike other boys. And it is through this process of retrospection that a beginning is found, the first murmurs of life as a gay person, a sign of things to come.

The early experiences of Darrell, who is today a thirty-nine-year-old longshoreman living in a small town on the Louisiana coast, illustrate the gay youth's sense of isolation.

> I remember when I was around eleven or twelve, I felt like I was strange, like everybody around me had it together except me, so I tried hard to fake it and fit in. But I still felt out of place a lot of the time, like I was out of step with everybody else. I don't know why. I didn't feel stupid or ugly or anything. Nobody called me names or made fun of me. . . . Now I see that I was gay and just didn't know it.
>
> When I started middle school, I met a boy named Landy and we became best friends. We spent all our time together. Back then, I didn't know just how close we were, but now I can see that I loved him, I guess you could say, in the way that boys that age love each other. I didn't know I was gay . . . only a lot later when I was in high school and other guys were getting into girls and I was still going for guys. . . . It's funny how it was right there in front of me all the time and I just didn't see it. I think everybody else saw it before I did.

While some gay youths remain out of touch with their sexual feelings well into adulthood, most, like Darrell, begin to take notice of them during their early teens. In one study, researchers found that homosexual boys, on the average, discover their attraction to other boys at the age of 12.8 years,[23] while another found thirteen years to be the norm.[24] Additional research has likewise found the early teens—twelve to fourteen years—to be the time when most gay youths begin to recognize their sexual urges, as well as to realize that these desires may spark resistance, even outright hostility, in others.[25] Of course, many straight youths experience sexual desires for their own gender during this time as well; such attractions are not necessarily confined to gay adolescents.

As for the later teenage years, Dr. Troiden questioned the participants in his study about the period between thirteen years of age and the point at which they graduated from high school, the usual age for this being seventeen to eighteen years. The result: two-thirds of them first engaged in sex with other boys to the point of orgasm when they were, on the average, 14.9 years old. Also at this age, their feelings of being different from others—feelings they had previously experienced as a vague sense of alienation—now crystallized into a sharp sense of sexual distinctiveness. In all, 99 percent remembered feeling "sexually different" during this period in their lives. They also recalled struggling with the possibility that they might be homosexual by the time they were seventeen years old.[26]

Reflecting on these feelings, many participants explained that, compared to nongay boys at the time, they were less interested in girls or found romantic relationships with them unfulfilling, while others attributed it to their realization that they were attracted to other boys. Eleven percent were already engaging in sex with other boys, and, for this reason, felt unlike their straight peers.[27]

Curiously, while most of the men in this and similar studies became aware of, and acted on, their homosexual urges at a relatively young age, the majority did not consider themselves to be gay at the time. Nearly always, several years elapsed before they identified themselves as such, a delay due, for the most part, to a constellation of societal and psychological forces that deflected their awareness away from this central truth about themselves. Yet even today, with adolescents defining themselves as homosexual at increasingly younger ages, such an identity is often arrived at only after a period of deep uncertainty and upon wrestling with a procession of antagonistic forces, both internal and external.

Societal Barriers to Self-Discovery

To be sure, myriad factors may hinder a youth's discovery of his same-sex nature, starting with society's expectation that he be reared as if he were straight. As we have noted, boys in our society are brought up to view themselves as heterosexual. Rarely, if ever, are they raised to think of themselves as gay. Even the child who is reared in such a way that effeminacy is unintentionally fostered in him—for instance, by parents who, wishing he were a daughter, inadvertently treat him as if he were a girl—is usually not expected to turn out gay. Rather, his mother and father count on him to grow into a heterosexual adult with a wife and children, this being the only sexual way of life sanctioned by mainstream society.

And it is true: other than celibacy in certain cases, such as in the priesthood, our principal social institutions accept no substitute for heterosexuality. Never has Western society endorsed, even briefly, other forms of sexual expression, namely bisexuality and homosexuality. Instead, our families, churches, business organizations, and governmental agencies, most conspicuously the military, have long championed the heterosexual orientation only, as if sexual disposition were a matter of choice, and heterosexuality, the correct selection. Even our educational system, which should be among society's most enlightened and progressive institutions, strives to indoctrinate youth into a heterosexist worldview, while treating in a disrespectful manner the student suspected of being gay.

In many elementary and secondary schools today, the pupil who is assumed to be homosexual is subjected to counterproductive measures. Rather than accepting his sexual orientation as a naturally occurring variation in sexual responsivity, school officials all too often interpret it as an aberration. Accordingly, they may caution or counsel him, notify his parents of their son's "problem," and make stringent efforts to redirect him back into the fold, as if requiring that he conduct himself in a conventionally heterosexual manner will somehow alter his genetic makeup and "cleanse" his personal history. Efforts to talk to and understand the boy, on the other hand, to respect the fact that he may be exceptional in this regard, are all too often missing. The aim, instead, is to compel him to somehow change his basic orientation or to at least pretend that it has changed. And it is in such ways, from infancy through adolescence, that boys are coerced into behaving as if they are straight when it is clear that they are not—compulsory social programming that may be deeply injurious to the gay adolescent.

In contrast, some of our more progressive educational institutions offer the services of school-based counselors for students who are believed to be homosexual, yet the counselors themselves may or may not be qualified to address the many complex issues involved in this orientation. Typically, they lack sufficient training in this area, a shortcoming that, when combined with their own sexual insecurities, may render them ineffective, if not downright harmful, to gay students.

Psychiatrist Emory Hetrick and his associate A. Damien Martin, whose work with homosexual youths is renowned, report that many adolescents have come to them for help after having first tried to discuss their concerns with school counselors who minimized or dismissed entirely the youths' concerns. "You are passing through a stage," some were told, or "that happens to lots of boys [girls]—it means nothing."[28] Others were advised, "you are too young to make up your mind," or, in the case of a fourteen-year-old girl, "you're too pretty to be a lesbian."[29]

To be sure, adolescent sexuality can be mercurial at times, and a youth will sometimes experiment with homosexuality even though he is heterosexual. It is for this reason, in fact, that the American Academy of Pediatrics emphasizes that teenage sexual behavior not be regarded as a foolproof predictor of adult sexual orientation.[30] Nevertheless, it is evident that many school counselors, as well as parents, cling to the notion that adolescent sexuality tends to be erratic in order to avoid facing a possibility that they find much more alarming—namely, that many youths are, and will remain, gay, and that they are not passing through a stage, but attaining a lasting insight into themselves.

And such denial on the part of these adults certainly does not help the adolescent himself. By failing to address the very real

likelihood that he may, indeed, be homosexual, they send him the
message that it is wrong to be gay, that being gay is something to be
avoided at all costs. And this, of course, only makes his adjustment
more difficult. Such a refusal to help him face and cope with reality
may delay and further confound his sexual and emotional development. No doubt, being forced to hide his same-sex orientation from
others—and quite possibly from himself—does not help the youth
recognize and come to terms with the unique nature of his sexual
impulses. In fact, the act of concealing these urges may, in itself,
produce unhealthy consequences.

"Every time a homosexual denies the validity of his feelings or
restrains himself from expressing, he does a small hurt to himself,"
writes Peter Fisher in his book, *The Gay Mystique: The Myth and
Reality of Male Homosexuality.*[31]

> He turns his energies inward and suppresses his own vitality.
> The effect may be scarcely noticeable; joy may be a little less
> keen, happiness slightly subdued, he may simply feel a little
> rundown, a little less tall. Over the years, these tiny denials
> have a cumulative effect.

Also over the years, the gay adolescent's sexual urges tend to
crest, spilling over into consciousness and creating waves of emotional turmoil. Of course, this is entirely predictable, given that the
youth may have heretofore had little reason to question his sexuality. The eruption of intense and seemingly inescapable same-sex
needs, then, may come as a most unwelcome surprise to him.

And the ensuing emotional crisis may be staggering. Certainly
the statistics speak for themselves: the suicide rate for gay teens is
double to triple that for straight ones, largely because of the additional burdens brought on by gay-related worries and concerns.
Besides struggling with the customary hurdles of adolescence—
finding acceptance within a peer group, learning to be intimate,
developing an identity distinct from one's family, planning a viable
future—the youth must also grapple with an orientation that family,
friends, teachers, and clergy may abhor, a distressing predicament
for a gay adult to face, let alone an adolescent who may be too
young to have developed the coping skills necessary to manage
such adversity.

In the *Report of the Secretary's Task Force on Youth Suicide*, Paul Gibson, a San Francisco therapist, identified several factors that may contribute to suicidal tendencies in homosexual adolescents.[32] Such a youth may have difficulty recognizing and accepting his same-sex orientation, for instance, perhaps feeling guilty because his religion teaches that it is sinful, and he may feel isolated as well, sensing rejection from his peers and a lack of emotional support from his family. Feeling alone and unloved and unable to accept himself, then, he may consider suicide.

"I wanted to strangle the entire straight world for making adolescence, which is hard enough for most people anyway, so much harder for people like me," said one teenage boy from Rhode Island.[33] "I think I will always carry the scars . . ."

Among the mountain of developmental tasks confronting such a youth is his need to reexamine his self-image, particularly his concept of himself as a sexual being. Having been raised to see himself as straight, the appearance of same-sex desires threatens to shatter his habitual way of viewing himself. To someone in this position, the presence of homoerotic yearnings may mean that he is not the person he thought he was, that he is somehow alien to himself, as well as the type of person his family and friends would be quick to condemn. For that matter, he might be quick to condemn himself if he were to determine that he is, in fact, gay.

Sometimes merely the possibility of having such an unpopular and unfamiliar orientation is enough to launch a person into a crisis. Fortunately, to help prevent one from spiraling into an emotional maelstrom, the human psyche has evolved in such a way as to activate an array of defense mechanisms, automatic mental processes that protect one from devastating emotional pain. When it comes to homosexual panic, however, these mechanisms most often work by eclipsing the individual's awareness of his same-sex nature, since it is this budding awareness that triggers the distress in the first place. Defense mechanisms, then, while dulling the person's emotional pain may, in the process, stall the coming-out process itself.

Emotional Barriers to Self-Discovery

The conflicted gay person may find his homosexual urges entirely absent, for instance, or present only in his dreams or fantasies, signifying that his discomfort with the whole matter has become so great that his sexual desires have been driven completely out of awareness. Of course, the individual remains homosexual; he just does not experience his erotic longings consciously. He may appear nonsexual as a result of this inhibition of desire, yet his sexual urges may still find gratification, albeit in roundabout ways.

Other individuals, while not forcing their desires out of consciousness, strenuously avoid contact with any article, book, film, or discussion involving homosexuality. Due to the person's exquisite sensitivity to the topic, anything that touches on this form of affection, even remotely, may trigger a stunning anxiety reaction.

It is also common for such a person to stay away from the gay districts of large cities and to avoid meeting gay people for the same reason. Encounters of this type are just too alarming. Yet some troubled individuals shy away for the opposite reason. Because direct contact with the gay world and its people would familiarize them with homosexuality, it might also diminish the panic that they associate with it. And that is the fear: as homosexuality becomes less intimidating, it might become more inviting.

Another method that an individual may use to reduce his anxiety is to convince himself this his attraction to his own gender is only temporary, a passing phase that he will "grow out of" someday. Or he may try to convince himself that his erotic desires are unimportant, if not trivial. "All guys are attracted to other guys," he'll insist. "We're all basically bisexual deep down." And while, technically speaking, he may be correct to some degree, he may nevertheless be placing far more weight on these facts than is warranted, manipulating them in such a way as to reduce the significance of his sexual nature rather than facing its importance in his life. By deflating his sexuality, however, he does diminish its power to provoke fear in him.

Still others push away unwanted desires by channeling them into innocuous activities. When this process is in operation, the person, without realizing it, diverts his sexual energies into endeavors such as the arts, athletics, or academia, the result being that his sex drive is markedly reduced and hence much less bothersome. Moreover, as a bonus, if he engages in such benign activities diligently, he may win acclaim and perhaps great success. This particular defense mechanism, then, is an intricate and sophisticated one, an elaborate process that may yield real-life gains.

Related to this, a gay person who cannot accept his sexuality may become an overachiever, throwing himself into a career with remarkable zeal in order to distance himself from his emotional conflicts and compensate for his feelings of personal inadequacy. His reasoning is that by proving to himself and others that he is adept in the career world, the fact of his homosexuality will be mitigated.

Lastly, the fearful individual may try to flee from his sexual yearnings by adopting the mindset and lifestyle of those who are popularly believed to represent the polar opposite of homosexuality. He may become excessively pious, for instance, or date ostentatiously and perhaps marry and produce a family. In this regard, research by Masters and Johnson reveals that approximately 25 percent of gay men marry women at one time or another, and we could speculate that, for some of these men, such unions are attempts to escape from their same-sex needs.[34] It is through a relationship of this type that a homosexual man's counterfeit "straight" identity is shored up, at least temporarily, as he "proves" to himself and others that he is incontestably heterosexual. Of course, the man remains gay and the astute observer may well see through the elaborate smokescreen, yet by enabling him to continue viewing himself as straight, this mental maneuver effectively diminishes the man's otherwise unmanageable anxiety.

A comparable process is at work when an insecure gay youth or adult becomes antagonistic toward gay people in general, railing against the presence of homosexuality in the world; in effect, making clear for all to see his fundamental opposition to same-sex affection. Sometimes such a person will even adopt a belligerently antigay stance and go so far as to physically attack those he believes to be gay, in this way fighting outwardly against that which he battles inwardly. This does not mean, however, that all gay bashers are gay; merely that some of them are homosexual and are struggling violently against facing this fact.

As for the use of defense mechanisms in general, the sexually conflicted person may unknowingly use any or all of the processes described here, but such strategies often prove unsuccessful in containing apprehension and doubt in the long run. Furthermore, even when they are effective, the person may still experience periods of anxiety and depression, a sense of ennui and aimlessness, and feelings of hopelessness about the future. In some cases, physical symptoms may also emerge, especially those that are stress-related, while in other cases, the person may simply feel bad without knowing why.

Of course, overwhelming confusion may set in, too, as the troubled person's defenses start to fail, and it is at such a time that he may finally begin to consider that he may be gay; a prospect requiring that he alter radically the way in which he thinks about himself, his relationships, and his future. It is also a point at which an individual typically launches a private, intense search for information about homosexuality.

The Quest for Information

For the individual faced with the possibility that he may be gay, the first order of business usually involves seeking out useful information. Knowledge is indispensable at such times. One study, in fact, found that 15 percent of gay men realize that they are homosexual as a result of reading books or other materials on the subject.[35] Unfortunately, most such reading matter, at least in years past, has been limited to "doctor books"—home medical encyclopedias—and lay texts on psychiatry, sources that have erroneously portrayed the same-sex orientation as a disorder.

Today, due to advances in our understanding of human sexual functioning, homosexuality is no longer classified as an affliction nor thought by those in the mental health profession to be a changeable condition. For that matter, most therapists do not consider a sweeping change in sexual orientation to be a realistic or a desirable goal. They find no compelling reason why a person should be heterosexual rather than homosexual.

Nevertheless, many sources of information persist in presenting the same-sex disposition in an unflattering light. Seldom are discussions of it comprehensive, being balanced with information about its benefits and possibilities. Instead, this remains an area in which our society is obstinate, one in which it is unwilling to part with entrenched, centuries-old bigotry.

To be sure, except for the gay press, there continue to be few ways that an individual who is unsure of his sexuality can learn objectively about life as a gay person, especially if he lives in a small town or rural area; society's reproachful stance discourages him from even inquiring. Instead, he is denied, in a variety of ways, the right to understand his own sexuality, with accurate and useful information being withheld from him on the grounds that it might "promote" homosexuality, as if knowledge were a malevolent force.

Since the person is already gay and will remain so, the only real effect of heavy-handed, oppressive tactics of this sort, if they have any effect at all, is that of perpetuating the person's confusion and undermining his mental health and spiritual well-being. What he needs is a safe emotional climate in which he can ask for and receive credible information, and in which he can sort through his feelings and come to terms with his innermost needs.

As it stands, most information that is readily available to gay youths today continues to be that which is disseminated by parents, friends, teachers, ministers, and the media, including the film industry, all of which are inclined to paint a woefully inaccurate picture of gay life. This is not surprising, though, considering that most of these sources are unlikely to have significant first-hand knowledge of the subject. Consequently, most adolescents know, in the technical sense, what a gay person is, but their images of such an individual are so badly distorted that it becomes unthinkable that they, too, might be gay. "I'm not like that!" a boy will protest when confronted with a stereotype of the homosexual man. And, in all likelihood, he is probably not like that. Few of us are.

Just a glimpse at the myths that society has affixed to homosexuality over the ages reveals just how farcical, and damning, these images can be. Researchers have reviewed various bodies of literature in search of popular misconceptions about gay individuals and have detected a history of distortions. In the seventeenth century, for instance, it was cautioned that the presence of homosexuality would bring "earthquakes, famine, pestilence . . . floods, and very fat, voracious field mice,"[36] while in our own century, gays have been cast as predatory creatures—"criminal seducers"—who are unable to form relationships other than those that are erotic and immature; as a threat to children, the family unit, and the human race itself; and as soft and underdeveloped, and thus unfit for demanding professions.[37] Homosexuality has been accused, as well, of ushering in a spectrum of social ills, including World War II and the Holocaust, the eating disorder *anorexia nervosa*, urban street crime, and even declining test scores on college entrance exams.[38] And today, the image of the gay man as an "AIDS carrier" is a special favorite among opponents of same-sex affection, most notably among those who cloak their bigotry in the mantle of religious fundamentalism.

Yet even those who are tolerant and socially progressive may, in all innocence, reduce gay men to cultural stereotypes. They may, for instance, think of them as glib individuals, as stimulating and provocative company, and a must for any dinner party guest list because they are so animated and amusing; in other words, the gay man as court jester. With such provincial and confining images associated with homosexuality, then, it is no wonder that the evolving gay person would fail to identify with this orientation. Characterizations like these simply do not mesh with who he is. They fail to reflect the depth and dimension of his life.

"I always thought of homosexuals as old men who walked poodles on rhinestone leashes and wore makeup," recalled a twenty-four-year-old man in *Two Teenagers in Twenty*, a collection of coming-out stories.[39] "I never thought, dreamed, or realized that there were, or ever had been, homosexuals who were my age."

Adds sociologist Barry Dank:

> If the societal stereotype of homosexuals is one of dirty old men, perverts . . . and so on, it should not be surprising that the young person with homosexual feelings would have difficulty in interpreting his experience in terms of the homosexual category.[40]

Unfortunately, this same young person may have little or no access to real gay youths and adults, the result being that he is unable to learn what such a person is really like. He may lack the opportunity to discover that most gay people are very much like himself, a state of affairs perpetrated, in large part, by the decisions of millions of productive gay citizens to keep their sexual orientations out of public view, including those whose achievements are truly exemplary.

Certainly there is, and has long been, a dearth of successful gay men who are comfortable presenting themselves forthrightly in society. In towns both large and small, stable, prosperous, and personally and professionally acclaimed homosexual men live closeted lives—they would say *discreet*—such that local gay youths know virtually nothing of their existence. The result is that only the more eccentric or stereotypic members of the gay community are visible, or perhaps just the lesbian segment, thereby providing the homosexual male youth with an inaccurate and incomplete picture of the spectrum of gay personalities and possibilities.

A related difficulty concerns the scarcity of information and support for the same-sex orientation that exists in the gay youth's home. Like most households, his family tends to avoid discussing male homosexuality, but on those occasions when it does, it is nearly always in harsh, prohibitive terms. And such an atmosphere of disapproval is unique to the gay minority. That is, while other disenfranchised groups may be the targets of persecution outside the home, within the family one normally finds a similarity of views, a sense of understanding and solidarity, and a sharing of suffering and indignation, all of which serve to sustain the emotional well-being of the family members. Additionally, the home environment may provide the minority child with a historical perspective on his group—a living education of sorts—as well as a sense of purpose and direction for the future.

Not so for the gay youth. His parents and siblings are typically heterosexual and therefore do not understand his orientation or relate to it in any meaningful way. If anything, they are openly hostile toward it. As a result, his home life may contribute mightily to his difficulty acknowledging, accepting, and accommodating his sexual nature.

However, there may be room for hope in this regard. Though most families persist in frowning on male homosexuality, with enhanced public awareness of its origins, prevalence, and normality, some are becoming more accepting of it. Furthermore, despite the relentlessly negative view of gay male sexuality held by mainstream society, as well as the ongoing drought of accurate information on the matter, there does appear to be a trend in some quarters toward improved resources for gay adolescents. The 1990s have witnessed an increase in the number of hotlines and counseling centers offering services to this segment of the population, for instance, services that include peer support groups in some cases. Likewise, electronic billboards and chatlines—Internet connections that allow an uncertain gay youth (or adult) to obtain reliable information, as well as to communicate with other homosexual individuals about common concerns—have become more accessible by personal computer. Of course, some use them simply to build friendships with other gay people, which in itself may be a very productive use of the system. It may help the person overcome, to some degree, the sense of isolation and loneliness that he may have been enduring. Hopefully, this trend toward electronic communication will continue until all gay people, especially youths, have easy access to such technology.

As it stands, however, many young people have neither computers in their homes nor progay resources in their communities, particularly those living in outlying areas: openly gay role models are usually nonexistent, as are gay community centers. Furthermore, conveying their concerns to their loved ones may seem entirely out of the question at this early point in the coming-out process, such that these youths may not know where to turn for guidance. Accordingly, they may turn directly to a gay community in a nearby urban area for answers. By meeting and talking to other gay people in relaxed, informal social settings, the curious individual can ask questions without fear of censure. In the company of those who are at ease with themselves, he can express his feelings and concerns secure in the knowledge that doing so will not trigger hysterical reactions. At present, talking directly to other gay people seems to be among the most favored methods of learning about one's own homosexual feelings.

Indeed, several studies have found that nearly half of all gay youths and adults decide that they may be homosexual as a result of excursions into the gay world. But this does not mean that they necessarily engage in sex as a part of their journeys. The fact is, 18 percent of homosexual males discover that they are gay before developing physical relationships with other males.[41] The sharing of knowledge that emerges from nonerotic contact, it would seem, is often enough to help the uncertain person better understand himself.

Other individuals become aware of their homoerotic desires by being in circumstances that bring these needs to the surface, most notably, all-male environments, such as college dormitories, barracks, correctional facilities, and monasteries—conditions that force the issue. In this regard, a 1971 study found that 19 percent of the gay men surveyed realized that they had strong homosexual impulses while they were in the armed forces, this during the Vietnam era when the draft was still in effect and female military personnel were largely excluded from combat zones.[42] Yet even today, with an all-volunteer system and a greater and more visible female presence, the armed forces still place the enlisted man in situations compelling him to face his deepest needs. Recalled a man who eventually determined that he was exclusively gay:

> I went into service at seventeen, mainly to get away from home. That's where I finished high school. Anyway, when I was in service I started to realize that I felt a sexual attraction for other men, that I was as strongly attracted to men as I was to women. I was engaged to be married at the time, so I passed the attraction off as being due to the circumstances—the loneliness and lack of female companionship. I rationalized my feelings as indicating feelings of deep friendship. But I couldn't seem to stop thinking about it.[43]

Accounts like this reveal the surprise, as well as the confusion, worry, and self-reproach, that servicemen may experience when their same-sex desires moor themselves in consciousness. Had the gentleman in the example above not been placed in such close proximity to other men and for long stretches of time, several more years might have elapsed before he became fully aware of his homosexual impulses.

Another circumstance in which a youth or adult may confront his same-sex needs occurs when he becomes involved in an intimate relationship with another male. It is not uncommon for a man to build an intense, long-term relationship with another man, yet not grasp that either one of them is gay. He may believe that their relationship is exceptional, that if it weren't for this one other person with whom he is so affectionate, he would not be involved with males at all. But when the relationship eventually dissolves and he finds himself forming comparable bonds with other men, it may finally strike him that he does, in fact, have pressing same-sex needs.

Even more commonly, a person will become aware of his orientation while in the midst of a homosexual relationship. A study by Canadian researcher Gary McDonald found that 22 percent of gay men discover that they are gay while actively engaged in a relationship with another man,[44] an insight that presumably stems from the person's inability to continue denying his homoerotic nature in the face of the obvious. The following narrative recounts a man's discovery of his sexual disposition through just such an encounter:

> I met a straight guy when I was in college. . . . As our friend-ship developed, I realized that I was falling in love with him and that I had never cared for anyone as deeply as I cared for him. I think he suspected the way I felt for him but I'm not sure. One night we were out drinking with a bunch of guys at a college bar. We both got rather high and when we returned to the dorm I went with him to his room. It was the beginning of a very beautiful night. I walked over to him, put my arms around him, and kissed him. He reciprocated. . . . He is now married and has a family. This incident led [to] a fateful resig-nation on my part that I was irrevocably gay. Due to the beauty of the experience, however, I was able to rid myself of any doubts I had regarding my being homosexual as negating the possibility of being a good person.[45]

The sort of information gained from intimate experiences like the one described above is not the same as that acquired from books, computers, or other sources. It is not factual information in the strict sense, but knowledge issuing from one's immediate feelings and needs. And yet it is entirely valid, coming as it does from direct personal experience.

STAGE 2: COMING OUT TO ONESELF

At this point in the process, the person must gather the courage to apply the knowledge that he has obtained about homosexuality to his own thoughts, feelings, and fantasies. And if he is capable of being unflinchingly honest with himself, he will recognize that he fits the technical definition of "homosexual."

As for the age at which this insight occurs, the late teens to the early twenties seem to be the most common time, according to studies conducted during the 1970s and 1980s.[46,47,48] More recent research, however, suggests that some people are now realizing that they are gay at even younger ages, a development due most likely to the growing availability of information on the subject, the increased visibility of the gay population, and society's greater tolerance of this sexual orientation. In effect, increased access to information about homosexuality allows young gay men to more quickly recognize their same-sex dispositions, something that may have taken them years longer when such facts were more aggressively stifled by society.

But this does not mean that a person today is any more pleased at the prospect of being gay than a person in the past. At best, he may feel relieved by finally facing this truth about himself; at worst, depressed and demoralized by it. For many people at this early stage, merely tolerating the fact that they are homosexual requires considerable effort. As we have noted, harsh societal attitudes instill such reactions.

In terms of the ways in which the individual may deal with this new self-knowledge, if he is an adolescent and still attending school, he may decide to withhold it from his classmates to protect himself from emotional and physical abuse. For the same reason, he may keep it from his parents and siblings, depending on his family's stability, attitudes toward homosexuality, and potential for violence. And there is no dishonor in doing this; it may be an essential survival tactic.

"Being in the closet can be absolutely necessary in certain situations," say Drs. Hetrick and Martin.[49] "Perhaps the most important coping strategy for the homosexually oriented adolescent is learning to hide." This means, though, that the youth must live in a constant state of vigilance, and this is neither a healthy nor a pleasant way to conduct one's adolescence.

And such ceaseless hiding may demand much of the person. "Gay adolescents are forever monitoring themselves," writes Dennis Anderson in the journal *Adolescent Psychiatry*.[50] "'Am I standing too close?' 'Is my voice too high?' . . . What should be spontaneous expressions of affection or happiness become moments of agonizing fear and uncertainty."

Drs. Hetrick and Martin concur:

> Individuals in such a position must constantly monitor their behavior in all circumstances. . . . [H]ow one dresses, speaks, walks, and talks become constant sources of possible discovery. One must limit one's friends, one's interests, and one's expression, for fear that one might be found guilty by association.[51]

For the same reason, a homosexual boy may publicly date girls, join in boisterous sports, or commit defiant or "macho" acts—anything to escape being perceived as gay. Recalled a man about his adolescent years:

> I spent all my time trying to keep up the image. You know, straight, solid, always in control of how people saw me or so I wanted to believe. What happened was I sacrificed those years trying to act straight, and now I can't go back and reclaim them. They're gone. . . . I wasn't really able to live my life back then, but what else could I do? I didn't see much of a choice.

In all, then, concealing one's sexual and affectional interests during this tumultuous period in life may be adaptive in that it protects the person from harm, yet maladaptive in that it requires him to relate to family and friends on the basis of deceit. Furthermore, covering up one's sexuality sooner or later generates more problems than it solves and is thus a style of coping that must ultimately be discarded. Yet after disguising his sexuality for such a long time, the person may find it extremely difficult to reverse directions and bring out into the open this very sensitive aspect of himself. Doing so may feel unnatural by this time, going against that which he has been obliged to do throughout his formative years—perform a masquerade—and causing him to feel vulnerable to rejection and abandonment.

Efforts to Change

To avoid such pain, the person may decide to take firm action, for instance, by attempting to transform himself into a heterosexual. To this end, he may seek professional help in changing his orientation, but may meet with little success in finding a therapist who will agree to assist him. As we have noted, therapists today are disinclined to view an individual's sexual disposition, heterosexual or homosexual, as a pliable condition or, for that matter, as something that should be changed. There is simply no sound reason why a man should be straight rather than gay. Instead, the person's difficulty with accepting such a basic part of himself is ordinarily seen as the real problem, with the goal of therapy being to help him view his sexual nature more reasonably, accept it more fully, and integrate it more completely into his life.

Others turn to religion for help, hoping that prayer, repentance, and sacrifice will bring about the desired change. "I prayed every day to have a sexual feeling for girls," recalled a young man from Seattle.[52] "I prayed that I would start liking sports. I prayed that I would stop watching sports just so I could look at the guys. But no change ever came."

Of course, this young man is not alone in this respect. For most, if not all, people who appeal to religion, there is also no change, at least not in the form of a new and different sexual orientation. And the result is sometimes a loss of faith.

Said the man from Seattle: "I felt that . . . I was no longer loved and protected by a God I had devoted my life to."[53]

As could be expected, when it becomes apparent that a pervasive change is not forthcoming, the troubled person may search for still other ways to suppress his homosexuality. He may, for instance, decide not to act on his desires. Either he pledges himself to lifelong celibacy or forces himself to form a heterosexual relationship as a "corrective" measure, in effect trying to rehabilitate himself as if he were disabled. But while such retraining may, at best, permit him to learn certain heterosexual techniques, it does not mean that his sexual or emotional needs for other men will wane or that an overwhelming passion for women will now overtake him.

Dave Pallone, a former umpire for the National League, addresses this issue candidly as he describes his struggle to interest himself in sex with women:

[I]t happened one night with a girl I was seeing casually. We had gone bowling and we were driving home in my father's car when I pulled off to a secluded spot so we could make out. . . . Well, it felt . . . okay. But not like it was supposed to feel. Even though it was the magical "first time," it wasn't rockets going off or the earth moving or even the car rolling. . . . It was strange; I found her attractive enough to be aroused, yet something was missing.[54]

Men in such circumstances do not understand that their sexual orientations will not change simply because they have sex with women. This would be akin to a straight man forcing himself to make love to another man: his heterosexuality would not vanish as a result. If anything, the whole experience might further assure him of his straightness.

And so it is for a gay man. Engaging in sex with a woman, rather than transforming him into a heterosexual, usually leads him to realize, more than ever before, that he is indisputably gay.

As for the course of such relationships between gay men and straight women, often they devolve into cold, barren unions characterized by listless, frustrating sex lives, and sooner or later collapse. Quite often they are unpleasant ordeals for both partners, including the woman who did not know that her lover was homosexual and that their relationship was, to some extent, illusory, and who may have wrongly blamed herself for the man's lack of interest in her and for the dissolution of the relationship itself.

At other times, a woman will become romantically involved with, and perhaps marry, a man with full knowledge that he is gay, and together they will attempt to redirect his sexual impulses into their relationship. And while such a union shows a certain integrity in that it is based on a forthright acknowledgment of the man's sexual nature, it still faces formidable odds. In some cases, the partners eventually find their relationship ungratifying and decide to separate, while in other cases, they restructure it so that they may be intimate with other people, in this way salvaging their alliance. In no event, however, does the man's sexual orientation actually change.

Still another way that an individual may attempt to adjust to his homosexuality is by allowing himself to have sex with males, while struggling to convince himself that such encounters do not mean that he is gay. "I only do it for the money," a hustler will claim, or "I just do it as a favor for friends," another will insist. "I'm not really gay, since I'm the 'active' partner," is a popular line used by insecure gay youths and adults, particularly those belonging to minority groups of certain types,[55] to assure themselves and others that they are not homosexual despite the evidence to the contrary.

Such attempts to explain away one's actions is similar to the tactic that we discussed earlier in which a troubled person tries to minimize the importance of his desires so that they will be less distressing to him. In the present case, however, which occurs further along in the coming-out process, the individual is not just downplaying his attraction to other males but is actually engaging in sex with them and trying to dilute the significance of these encounters. By this point, he usually recognizes that he has same-sex needs, but still clings to the notion that he is predominantly straight.

A similar theme runs through the "victim" defense, examples being, "he seduced me," and "I'm gay but I can't help it, it's my parents' fault." Here the person is allowing that he is homosexual but is attributing it to someone or something beyond his control. By absolving himself of causing or choosing his sexuality, he believes that he releases himself from any responsibility for it. He may thus be intimate with other men without guilt or self-reproach.

As with other efforts to justify or defend his same-sex orientation—which, at this point, the person still feels he must do—the victim defense is usually temporary. As he becomes more at ease with his homosexuality, his need to hold others accountable for it diminishes or disappears entirely.

STAGE 3: EXPLORATION AND EXPERIMENTATION

Besides taking responsibility for his sexuality, as a person becomes more comfortable being gay he may also experience a growing curiosity about gay life. As a result, he may decide to increase the number and types of encounters he has with other men, sexual or otherwise, which marks the beginning of the exploratory stage of the coming-out process. This is a step that can occur at any age, the criteria being that the person finally acknowledges, at least to himself, that he does indeed have same-sex impulses and that he wishes to pursue this new discovery.

Of course, one of the simplest ways that a man may meet other gay men is by entering into a setting, such as a gay community, that accepts homosexuality wholeheartedly. It is here that the individual, for perhaps the first time in his life, is not only free to be openly attracted to other men, but actively encouraged to form amicable bonds with them. For this reason, the gay world may at first seem paradisiacal to the inexperienced homosexual man who may be eager to indulge in long-held fantasies, especially if he has endured years of fear and hiding and a lifelong drought of same-sex affection.

But there are exceptions. To the man who is well into adulthood by the time he embarks on the coming-out process, particularly the one who is middle-aged or beyond, experimentation with gay life may cause him to feel that something is amiss within him, that he is behaving like an adolescent. And, indeed, a man who sets out on the coming-out process at an advanced age may well be mature and responsible in most every respect, yet conduct himself like a youth when it comes to sex, enthusiastically dating several men and trying on different roles. This is because, in a very real sense, he is only now going through the sexual adolescence that he was required to forgo earlier in his life. And this is a normal, predictable occurrence. Just as the developing straight youth has a healthy need to explore his sexuality, so too does the evolving gay person, regardless of the age at which he discovers his sexual disposition. And such experimentation is important for several reasons.

For one, it allows the person to acquire sexual knowledge, an essential step for those of all orientations, as well as to develop certain nonsexual, social abilities. Since a boy who is attracted to other boys is rarely allowed to date them, he has no way of developing the skills necessary to build and sustain healthy, intimate relationships with other males. Whereas heterosexual youths are groomed for dating and marital roles as a routine aspect of their education—the high school prom being but a dress rehearsal for the straight adult world—homosexual adolescents are denied this sort of guidance and practice. They are not shepherded into constructive, acceptable gay roles and, therefore, may end up delayed in the social realm. It is during the exploratory stage, then, that they may, at last, catch up.

Thus, by making contact with the gay world, the individual may learn how to socialize with other men and form affable bonds with them, enhancing both his self-confidence and his prospects of forming productive relationships in the future. He may also firm up his identity as a gay man and experiment with any behaviors, conventional or otherwise, that he was not allowed to engage in previously.

Some gay men, for instance, are ridiculed for being effeminate, yet likewise mocked when they attempt to behave in a more masculine manner. They have been relegated to the role of "sissy" and are expected to stay within that role. Once the person has extricated himself from such oppressive circumstances, however, and is in a healthier environment, he may wish to test out certain masculine behaviors to see how they feel. And in so doing, he may find that they better suit his personality.

Other men prefer to experiment with feminine characteristics and interests. In some cases, this is because the person is merely curious about such things, while in other cases it is because he feels intuitively drawn toward the feminine. In still other cases, it is because the individual has been brought up to believe that this is how gay men act; thus, he is attempting to conform to a cultural stereotype.

Addressing this latter reason, Drs. Hetrick and Martin report that, in their work with gay adolescents, they have found that some of those who experiment with cross-dressing quit doing so once they meet other homosexual youths who do not dress like the opposite sex.[56] The implication is that some youths cross-dress not because it expresses their personalities, but because they mistakenly believe that, as gay individuals, this is what they are supposed to do. Exposure to the gay world, then, may help them recognize and rectify this and other misconceptions.

In addition, venturing into the gay community may help the person realize that, as a group, homosexual men cannot be pigeonholed; that each one is unique in his own way; that it is neither necessary nor desirable for all gay men to think or look or act alike; that the diversity of the homosexual population is one of its greatest assets and, as such, should be respected, protected, and nurtured. And the converse is also true: exploring the gay world may help a person realize that there are many other gay people out there who are very much like him in key respects, with a common result being that the individual at last discards his negative views of homosexuality and replaces them with a more precise picture of what it means to be gay. That is to say, he redefines the meaning of the term so that it becomes more inclusive; it becomes a group to which he, himself, comfortably belongs.

STAGE 4: COMING OUT TO OTHERS

By this point, the evolving gay person usually finds himself wishing to tell others about his orientation. It may even be a pressing need now.

When he was younger and did not know for sure that he was gay, he may have hidden his sexual concerns from his family and friends. And this is entirely understandable. But once the person realizes that he is definitely gay, especially if he feels rather good about it and wishes to live openly as a gay man, he may yearn to tell those to whom he feels closest about this fundamental feature of himself. For that matter, not telling them might cause him to feel deceitful; it might make him feel that his relationships are fraudulent in that they are based on information that he now knows to be false. Personal integrity, then, becomes the driving force.

Of course, besides allowing him to live according to his principles, revealing himself in this way also closes forever the chasm between his private self and his public self, bringing into line the way in which he views himself and the way that others perceive him. And this, in itself, is the ultimate coping strategy, since it addresses the conflict directly and resolves it permanently. By correcting others' misperceptions of him, the discomfort that the man has endured for such a long time abates. He no longer must pretend, no longer must feel that he is living two irreconcilable lives, and no longer must worry about being discovered and accused of dishonesty. And the result may be a deep sense of relief.

Richard Troiden, the researcher whose work we discussed earlier, queried the men in his study about their emotional states before and after coming out and found that nine out of ten reported that they were "more happy" after they had finally dealt with their homosexuality.[57] Another study looked at men who came out to their spouses and found that, after disclosing their same-sex orientations and going on to build lives compatible with their same-sex dispositions, these men reported enhanced self-esteem and improved physical health.[58] Clearly, being candid about one's sexual nature, while perhaps precarious in the beginning, does allow a person to throw off a heavy emotional burden, the eventual outcome being a sense of respite, well-being, and self-respect.

Of course, the first order of business is to decide who to come out to and how best to do it. As one might expect, the gay individual may decide to first reveal himself to someone else who is gay. This may be because he assumes that this other individual already knows, perhaps because they met in the gay community or had a passing sexual encounter of some sort, and therefore feels that it would be reasonable for them to discuss such matters together. At other times, it may be because he needs advice about how to tell heterosexuals about himself and decides to ask someone who has already exited the closet.

As for the first straight person he tells, typically it is a close friend. Either he tells this individual directly or else drops a hint, in this way encouraging the friend to begin thinking about the matter and, hopefully, ask about it at some point. And the way in which the friend reacts to the announcement may be critical, since the gay person may interpret it, rightly or wrongly, as a predictor of the way in which others will respond to the news.

If, for instance, the friend becomes distant, hostile, or rejecting, then the gay person's coming-out process may suffer a serious setback. If, on the other hand, the friend responds in a thoughtful, accepting manner, then the homosexual individual, heartened by the support, may be more inclined to come out to others in the future. Recalled Antonio, a twenty-five-year-old graduate student:

> I remember telling my friend David I was gay. He said it was okay. He said it didn't surprise him, he thought I might be gay. . . . I felt good after it was over. We joked about it for a few days. . . . It made me feel like it would probably be all right to tell some other people, but it was awhile before I did.

After telling a close friend, the person may proceed to tell another friend or perhaps a trusted brother or sister and, at some point, may consider coming out to his mother and father as well. And yet, while the parents are occasionally among the first people told, more often they are among the last. In fact, a certain portion of gay sons never come out to them at all, their parents' attitudes toward homosexuality being so contemptuous that an emotionally and perhaps physically volatile reaction is anticipated. Other sons, however, do take the chance, using the disclosure as an opportunity to educate their families about the same-sex orientation. Ultimately, the decision depends on the person's relationship with his father and mother, the reactions that are expected, and perhaps other factors, like financial considerations and housing needs. In the next chapter, we discuss in detail the coming-out process as it relates to the family.

STAGE 5: COMMITMENT AND INTEGRATION

Finally, once the man has gained sufficient sexual and emotional experience and is comfortable with, and forthright about, his sexuality, he may find himself wishing to settle into a relationship with another man.[59,60] By this time, he feels confident in his love-making abilities and possesses the social skills necessary to build and sustain meaningful relationships. Also, he may no longer find brief encounters entirely satisfying. This is because the spontaneous tryst, while sexually exciting and perhaps even genuinely loving and growth enhancing, nevertheless precludes other types of intimate needs from being met. By definition, impromptu encounters are transitory, such that any human need that depends on the enduring presence of another person cannot be entirely gratified by them. And one such need is companionship, along with emotional security and a sense of continuity in one's life—the desire for home and hearth, a need felt by many men regardless of sexual orientation.

Also during this stage, the man may find himself wishing to become involved in the political arena. Having long known the disapproving manner in which society views its homosexual members, then having experienced gay life first-hand and witnessed the harsh effects of this same attitude, his social conscience may impel him to act. Besides committing himself to a long-term relationship, then, he may devote himself to political action as well.

Of course, some gay men do not wish to become enmeshed in political activities of any sort, and this is their prerogative. Contrary to the position of many activists, not every gay person is obliged to participate in the struggle for gay causes just because he happens to be homosexual. The fact is, some men are grappling with other matters in their lives and have little time or energy left for political concerns. Others are not wrestling with any issues in particular, but are merely apolitical. Nevertheless, many gay people are fervently committed to social change. Having beheld the flagrant injustices perpetrated on this benign segment of the citizenry, they feel, at some point in their personal evolution, an overpowering need to speak out, a responsibility to act. And this is *their* prerogative.

Speaking out is also a part of "gay pride." Having accepted his sexuality and perhaps gained a heightened political awareness in the process, the individual may now find himself feeling a sense of dignity as a gay man. Not only does he no longer wish to conceal or change his orientation, he wishes to live it openly, with distinction. He may also take well-deserved pride in having accomplished an arduous and time-consuming feat: coming to grips with membership in a vilified minority.

To be sure, there is a large number of men who have accomplished the coming-out process and who are truly glad to be homosexual, honored to be among the ranks of gay men and women. And this often appears to be one indication that a person has progressed far in accepting his sexual orientation: a natural affinity for all other homosexual individuals by virtue of the fact that they are gay. What he can now accept in himself, he can also value in others. And even though he may have had little, if any, direct contact with an organized gay subculture, the man understands intuitively that most other gay people have, at one time or another, been the victims of persecution, ridicule, and hatred, and he empathizes with their plight. And such kinship with the entire gay population, such compassion for the collective, is one sign of the mature homosexual man.

Another is his ability to place his sexual disposition in perspective. During the years when he was struggling to accept his orientation, it may have been necessary for the man to invest the matter of his sexuality with much time and energy, such that this one component of his personality became amplified to the point of eclipsing other essential features. Once he reconciles himself to his homoerotic nature, however, his sexuality may become less of a concern.

He may now find himself incorporating it, naturally and spontaneously, into his overall self-image until he achieves a more complete identity, that of a fully functioning person, his sexuality woven into the larger tapestry of characteristics, traits, and predilections that comprise his being. Thus, his personality is now in a more integrated state in which its various aspects work together in greater harmony, producing within him a clarity of vision, an inner certitude, and a sense of personal liberation far surpassing that which he had previously known. And yet, despite his progress in this regard, the coming-out process must continue—in fact, it may never be entirely finished—since the man will likely find himself confronted from time to time with novel circumstances that require him to decide, yet again, whether he wishes to reveal to others his sexual orientation and how best to do it. By this point in his development, however, he has typically established a secure emotional foundation and a rich base of experience from which to make such a decision and is thus, more than ever before, truly in command of his life and his future.

SUGGESTIONS

The following suggestions may be helpful if you or someone you care about is in the process of coming out. They consist of general comments about the five stages of the process, as well as information about when and where to seek assistance if complications arise along the way.

1. Regarding the stages of the coming-out process, be aware that they do not always proceed in the sequence described in this chapter. Once in a while, the stages may overlap or their order may change. A person may come to terms with his homosexuality, for instance, and may disclose it to his friends and family before actually going out and exploring the gay world, assuming that he has the opportunity and the desire to explore it. Or a man may be openly gay and quite comfortable with his sexuality yet become reluctant, perhaps for good reason, to present himself candidly to others when called upon to do so in a new social situation. Accordingly, he may temporarily return to an earlier stage of development and guard his orientation. The process described in this chapter, then, should be

thought of as a general model, a prototype. In your own life, and depending on an array of factors, coming out may be somewhat less orderly than what is described in these pages.

2. Understand, too, that it is possible for a person to become stuck in one stage of the process and remain there for quite some time, even indefinitely. Some individuals stay in a permanent state of denial, for instance, conducting their lives as *faux* heterosexuals and never facing the truth about themselves. Others, though small in number, recognize that they are gay, yet hide this fact from the world and never develop an emotionally or physically intimate relationship with another person, male or female. Still others accept their same-sex needs but stay in the exploratory stage, initiating countless brief encounters in a revolving-door sex life while remaining emotionally unfulfilled.

Should you find yourself bound to one stage, particularly an early stage, and feeling frustrated by it, then consider seeking assistance. By doing so, you may free yourself to move forward.

3. If your concern over your sexual orientation becomes so great that you feel overwhelmed, you may find relief by contacting a gay hotline or similar resource. Today there are many phone services and counseling centers that exist expressly for this purpose; therefore, you should have little difficulty locating one. In addition, the Appendix contains a comprehensive listing of gay resources that you may contact for assistance.

4. If you are in your teens and are confused about your sexual orientation, remember that it is natural to be curious about, even perplexed by, sexual matters during this period in your life. This is entirely normal. If you are seriously troubled by them, however, consider talking to someone you know and trust or contacting a source like those mentioned above. Moreover, if you air your concerns to someone who responds by rejecting you, by dismissing your worries as unimportant, or by telling you not to be bothered by them because you will outgrow them, then find someone else to talk to, someone who is more comfortable and skillful discussing sensitive personal matters.

5. Finally, if you are heterosexual and someone with whom you have a close relationship tells you that he is gay, be supportive.

Thank the person for trusting you enough to share this important personal information with you, and do your best to deal with it constructively. Bear in mind that you may be the only person he has told, or perhaps only one of a handful, and that you are thus in a privileged and responsible position. Realize, too, that your reaction may have a very powerful impact on the person and that you should therefore respond as thoughtfully and supportively as possible in order to help him on his journey.

Chapter 2

The Family Sphere:
Gay Sons, Husbands, and Fathers

A nearly universal characteristic of those who are gay is a reluctance, at least initially, to come out to their families, with a sizable segment of the homosexual population never coming forward to their loved ones at all. A 1989 survey, for instance, found that roughly 20 to 40 percent of its gay sample had not shared this important personal information with their families.[1] And these are not just the shy types. Even the person who is otherwise outspoken may clam up when it comes to talking to his family about his same-sex orientation, which is disheartening given that one's affectional and sexual nature is such an important part of his personality, as well as a quality that may color nearly every aspect of his life. So why the silence?

By way of explanation, some men say that they have always felt uncomfortable talking to their families about sexual matters of any sort, let alone homosexuality, a sensitive topic in most households. Others fear that if they come out, they might end up immersed in guilt if the announcement should hurt or disappoint their loved ones. Still others say their families have made it clear that they do not want to know when a relative is homosexual. And some remain in the closet because they fear that their loved ones will reject them if they do not, even though these same gay individuals may participate publicly in gay-related political events designed to provoke the mainstream population. When scorn comes from within one's own family, however, it can be excruciating.

In this chapter, we look at these and other reasons for not being up front with one's family. We also explore the issues that arise when a person *does* come forward—specifically, when a son tells his mother and father that he is gay—and review two studies of the ways in which his parents are likely to respond. And we discuss a similar circumstance: the process that is set into motion when a homosexual husband and father comes out to his wife and children, nearly always a stunning revelation. The chapter concludes with suggestions for the gay person who is considering telling his relatives about himself, as well as advice for the family members themselves.

REASONS FOR NOT TELLING THE FAMILY

The justification that a person offers for not coming out to his loved ones may be either the result of a serious consideration of the pros and cons of making the disclosure or simply an excuse to avoid an unpleasant scene. Here we explore the reasons most often offered by those who decide to continue concealing their same-sex orientations.

Awkwardness of the Situation

As we have noted, some gay men explain that their families do not discuss sexual matters, ever. "We just don't talk about things like that," a person will say. And there may be a great deal of truth to this claim. Many families do have certain topics around which they artfully skirt, with human sexuality sometimes being among the most forbidden. And when it comes to male homosexuality in particular, the taboo may be especially strong. In fact, the whole issue of same-sex love may be entirely off-limits, such that any attempt to introduce it into a family discussion is regarded as crass and thoughtless and met with stern resistance.

For the gay person, however, the concern may be less that he will appear tactless than the fact that he does not know how to bring up the subject in the first place. Having never discussed real-life sexual matters with his loved ones, he has no prior experience to draw on, causing him to feel awkward, inept, and anxious. As a result, he finds himself putting off the announcement.

He may worry, too, that his family will be shocked. Indeed, if he does launch into such a discussion, some of his loved ones may well be startled. But merely because the topic has not been broached in the past or because it might surprise certain types of people does not mean that it should be side-stepped. While raising the issue may violate an age-old family taboo and perhaps offend certain types of individuals, it may still be the wisest course of action. This seems to be the conclusion of many gay people. While coming out may mean placing loved ones in an awkward circumstance, the disclosure itself is deemed important enough to warrant it. In fact, it may be absolutely essential if the person is to continue living and functioning healthily within the family. Causing shock to loved ones, then, becomes less of a concern as the individual realizes it is for a good reason.

In other cases, the person's family may not only shy away from discussions of human sexuality in general, but may let it be known that they prefer, if not insist, that the gay person in particular not divulge his orientation. Occasionally, this is expressed explicitly, but it may also be conveyed in a more subtle manner; for instance, by family members lapsing into a stony silence whenever the topic of same-sex love arises. Regardless of how it is expressed, though, the person soon learns that the rules of the game require that he keep quiet and act as if he is sexless, or better yet, pretend that he is straight. He comes to realize that he is expected to participate in a convoluted game of deceit, a strained and altogether unnecessary conspiracy of silence, and to do this out of respect for his loved ones' straight sensibilities, never mind the family's lack of respect for his own integrity.

But what is curious and frustrating about some of these same families is that once the gay person is out of earshot, his relatives openly discuss their suspicions of him. Although the family is unwilling to deal with the subject candidly with the individual present, pretending that the matter is distasteful and unfit for discussion, behind the person's back it becomes Topic A. This is a counterproductive way of handling the situation in that it disallows the target of gossip his rightful voice. Consequently, the gay person, confronted with such foolishness, may decide to stop submitting to the family's edict that he be mute and instead speak forthrightly about himself, in this way cleaning up a muddled family situation, while at the same time providing a model of healthy communication.

In other instances, denial or anger may be at the root of the silence. Either the parents cannot cope with the thought of homosexuality and therefore feel unable to discuss it with their son or else they are angry at him simply because he is gay and are trying to punish him by refusing to talk about the matter. In either case, the result is the same: an obstruction arises that prolongs a painful family situation.

The Desire to Protect from Pain

A second reason that a person may decide not to open up to his family is that he does not want to cause his loved ones any discomfort. He may believe that the disclosure will hurt them emotionally, something he wishes to avoid even at the expense of keeping concealed such an integral part of himself. For that matter, he may feel guilty merely because he is homosexual, such that the thought of now creating discomfort in his loved ones because of his gayness only increases his sense of self-reproach. And while the presence of guilt indicates that the person has not yet come to terms with his sexual nature, his wish to shield his family from emotional distress does speak well for his sensitivity and thoughtfulness, since many family members do indeed experience marked displeasure upon learning that a loved one is gay, especially when that person is in the immediate family. Still, several issues emerge when one uses this reason as the sole justification for keeping his sexual orientation under wraps.

The truth is, while members of some families do have difficulty handling the idea of homosexuality, most are not so delicate that they collapse merely upon learning that there is a gay person in the family. In most cases, our loved ones are more resilient than we assume, more able to cope with stress.

Furthermore, we must all, at times, share sensitive information with those we love. This is a fact of life. If we do not, we may inadvertently create a whole new set of problems for ourselves and others: perpetuating lies and half-truths, wrestling with feelings of self-reproach, and short-circuiting our relationships with those we love.

As it stands, too many gay people respect other peoples' feelings more than they respect their own, at times being much too selfless for their own good. In some cases, this is because the person was brought up to think primarily in terms of the needs of others, while in other cases it is because his self-esteem is very low, perhaps because he was treated so badly in the past that he has had little opportunity to develop respect for himself and his own feelings and needs. For years, he may have anguished over the caustic remarks and actions of those in his family, yet may find it unthinkable that he must now create discomfort in these same people. "Who am I to make them feel bad?" he asks.

Fortunately, some of these individuals eventually overcome this dilemma. They realize that they are valuable persons in their own right and that they have a legitimate reason for creating tension in their families under certain circumstances. Accordingly, they come out to their loved ones.

In still other cases, a person believes that while his family can probably cope with the news of his gayness, there is nevertheless a particular person who will be so anguished by the disclosure that it will result in lasting problems. And it may be true, there may be a certain family member who will have profound difficulty adjusting to the information.

"I was hysterical," said a mother of a gay child.[2] "I spent two days in bed mentally hysterical. In the past I had never retreated to bed over anything." Worse still, some family members' reactions last far longer than two days, enduring instead for a protracted period of time and creating problems for all concerned.

Often, an overreaction of this type occurs because the family member is in the dark about homosexuality, mistakenly equating it with mental disorder or moral depravity, misconceptions that may need to be corrected before a more reasonable reaction can take place. At other times, the family member may harbor secret concerns, such as the fear that he or she may be homosexual, too. Says a man who found out that he had gay relatives:

> For awhile there I wondered if homosexuality ran in the family. I have a brother who is gay and a son who is gay. I thought, "Am I sure I'm totally straight?" It very definitely bothered me for awhile. Now I've reached the point where I see no reason to question my own sexuality. I don't think it's bad to have a gay son or a gay brother anymore.[3]

To be sure, discovering that someone in the family is homosexual—particularly a person of the same gender—may be unsettling to the individual who already has sexual doubts and conflicts. And once such conflicts are open, they may be difficult to suppress, especially since they may resurface whenever the gay relative comes near. Consequently, loved ones who have not faced and resolved their own same-sex urges may be especially rejecting of the homosexual family member, as well as upset by the fact that he even brought up the subject in the first place.

In addition to relatives who are afflicted with homophobia, there may also be the loved one who is upset by the disclosure simply because his or her general mental condition is so shaky. A person having a history of mental disorder, for instance, could conceivably have a grossly distorted reaction upon finding out that a loved one is homosexual, with the inner turmoil triggered by the revelation intensifying the individual's already precarious emotional state.

Similarly, a loved one may be of sound mental health but, due to life circumstances, is currently under considerable stress. For this reason, the gay person, aware of the importance of proper timing, postpones the announcement until the relative's situation has stabilized.

A loved one might also be quite elderly and perhaps seriously ill. As a result, the homosexual individual decides not to come out to this relative at all, concerned that the disclosure might cause the person to become upset, possibly worsening his or her medical condition. This may also be the case when there is reason to believe that the relative will probably not have available the time needed to complete the adjustment process, a process that can take years.

In all, then, several factors, some of which may be unique to one's family, must be taken into account when considering whether and how to come forward to loved ones. As we have seen, the disclosure of one's homosexuality often sparks a complex and protracted response in the family network; therefore, any factor that could significantly affect this complicated process should be weighed carefully in advance.

Fear of Criticism, Rejection, or Assault

A third reason that a person may refrain from telling his loved ones about his orientation is because he fears that their reactions will crush him. He will say that he does not believe he could bear their contempt since it would come from those who have long been instrumental in his life and whose affection and approval are essential to him. He will say that he plans to wait until he feels better able to fend off their rebukes.

As could be expected, though, many people never reach such a point. Though they may be relatively immune to antigay affronts from individuals outside the family, they remain acutely sensitive to the opinions of those within it. And yet, some gay people, with time, do become better able to cope with familial disapproval. They gain self-awareness, as well as tenacity, and in the process learn to cope remarkably well with unfavorable comments from their loved ones. As a result, they eventually come out to them.

Of course, the fear of criticism may be most intense in the person who is emotionally dependent on his loved ones, the one who has an overarching need for uninterrupted emotional support and the sense of belonging that a family often provides. Though he may be receiving his family's affection on false pretenses, the person clings to it just the same because he is so reliant on it. Without his family's ongoing nurturance, life might seem unbearable to him. To such an individual, then, the risk of losing his emotional ties with his loved ones by coming out to them does not seem worth the price it would exact from him, perhaps causing him to spiral into a disabling state of anxiety and despair. Instead, he may first need to overcome some of his excessive dependence before he risks telling them about himself.

At other times, a youth or adult will conceal his sexual disposition not only because he is sensitive to his family's criticism, but also because he fears that the disclosure might lead to a permanent rejection. And this may be a realistic concern. Certainly there are those families that do disown any member who is different, especially one who is homosexual. This may be because the gay person is considered an embarrassment, the family's values being such that maintaining a conventional image in the community is considered more important than rallying around a relative who diverges from the norm. Or it may be because the family, due to ignorance or inflexibility, simply rejects homosexuality out of hand.

Which brings us to the question, "Should a person tell his family that he is gay if he has reason to expect a lasting rejection?" In some instances, an individual will anticipate the worst from his loved ones, fearing a resounding renunciation that will last a lifetime when, in reality, this is unlikely to happen. At such a moment, the person may be viewing the situation as he did when he was a child and felt small and powerless before his family. With reflection, he may come to realize that his anxieties are overblown, and may thus decide to venture forth and tell his family about himself.

In other cases, though, the person's fears may be on the mark, with his loved ones being very likely to denounce him. And if there is something substantial to be gained by remaining on good terms with them—present or future material gain, for instance—then he may decide to continue hiding his homosexuality. Depending on the circumstances, however, this may require that he sacrifice his integrity, a difficult task for a person of principle.

Of course, he *can* make the opposite choice, forgoing financial security or other types of advantage in order to open up to his family. And to the individual who does so, being honest is worth it. This sort of person usually takes the position that he does not need material or other types of gain so much that he is willing to betray himself to acquire it, nor does he see the point in remaining involved in a family that will not welcome him as he is; that if he must perform a masquerade to be accepted, then he is not really being accepted at all, that what is being embraced is a false image. And this is meaningless to him.

Even more worrisome than being rejected, however, is the predicament of the person who may be physically assaulted. When a family holds an inordinately harsh attitude toward homosexuality, and when there seems to be a very real likelihood that the gay person will be violently attacked if he reveals his orientation, then divulging it is probably not a wise move. In such a case, the individual should ask himself why he wishes to tell his loved ones. What is to be gained besides the satisfaction of knowing that he is being truthful? Or put another way: Is this honesty or is this poor judgment?

There will always be that individual who, knowing that a family member will probably assault him, comes out anyway. More often, however, as he is growing up, the gay person develops a repertoire of survival skills, among them the wisdom not to reveal himself to those who may be potentially dangerous to him. Rather, he waits until a more suitable time, a time when such people no longer pose a direct threat to his safety and well-being. Certainly this is a valid reason for withholding the disclosure.

Ultimately, some degree of risk will nearly always be present whenever a person comes out to his family, be it emotional, social, or physical. To be sure, predicting the reactions of loved ones to this particular piece of information is often a very difficult call, as we shall see in the next section.

TELLING ONE'S PARENTS

Among the family members whom the gay person must decide whether to tell about his sexual orientation, the most intimidating may be his mother and father. If a son does decide to open up to them, research tells us that they will almost certainly react negatively at first, with their emotions ranging from sadness and guilt to worry and anger. In the majority of cases, a combination of several painful feelings emerge. Moreover, the inner turmoil triggered by the announcement takes most parents a long time to get over—two years, by one estimate[4]—a fact that a son may not know when he comes out to them. Conscientious and concerned, he may yearn to be forthright with his father and mother and may believe that they, too, would want him to be straightforward about the matter.

The Decision to Disclose

As for the way in which a son may decide to let his parents know about himself, the disclosure can be approached in any number of ways. However he decides to do it, though, it remains a very personal matter; there are no definitive answers about precisely when and how it should be done. Certainly, it can be a very complicated undertaking, with an important consideration being the reason that he is considering doing it in the first place.

Presumably, most sons tell their parents because they want to be honest with them. It is often that simple. The son's integrity compels him to come out to those he loves and respects. In fact, not doing so may cause his relationships with them to feel unreal, partial, and deceitful.

In other cases, a son realizes that his mother and father will eventually deduce that he is gay anyway; that it is difficult, if not impossible, to keep secret forever something as fundamental as one's sexual orientation, particularly when the years of bachelorhood begin to mount. He comes out, then, because he feels that it is inevitable. Moreover, by choosing the circumstances in which he does it, he exercises a degree of control over the affair.

Still other sons come forward because they are tired of living two separate lives. Camouflaging one's true sexual nature can become increasingly tedious over the course of time, especially when one is content being gay. To the well-adjusted homosexual man, concealing his sexual disposition from his parents may sooner or later begin to feel ludicrous.

Of course, the presence of a lover or life partner may be another reason for opening up. When a son develops a devoted relationship with another man—particularly when they decide to create a home together—it may become necessary to inform the parents. How else to explain the presence of this new person? And yet, a son may make the disclosure not only because his same-sex orientation is now much more apparent, but also because he is genuinely proud of his relationship with this special individual in much the same way that a happily married heterosexual man may take pride in his wife and in their life together. Understandably, the gay son believes that to deliberately misrepresent his union with his lover as being "just friends" or "roommates" would insult his partner and violate the heart of their relationship. Accordingly, out of love and respect, he refuses to engage in such a bald betrayal, thus making it imperative that he come out to his parents.

A son may tell his father and mother, too, because of medical reasons. He may develop HIV illness, for instance, and feel that he should share this information with them, especially if he has progressed to the point of displaying visible symptoms of the condition. In such a case, he may find himself in the unenviable position of having to disclose to them both that he is homosexual *and* HIV-infected, no doubt a difficult task.

Lastly, a son may make the announcement for a far less noble reason: to wound his parents. Here the revelation tends to spill out in the heat of a family quarrel and is intended to startle, appall, and enrage. And it usually does. But this is a dubious reason for coming out, as well as one of the worst possible ways of doing it, since it sets the stage for a long-standing negative attitude toward the son's sexual orientation. Fortunately, the desire to hurt their parents rarely seems to be the reason that sons reveal this information to them.

In terms of the act of coming out itself, care should always be taken regardless of how the disclosure is approached. This is serious information and is usually received as such by the parents, especially when the son is young. Most how-to manuals, in fact, as well as journal articles by those who counsel gay youths and their families, advise caution. They try to help the young reader anticipate the possibility of the bitter consequences that the disclosure may bring. Having witnessed the sometimes tragic effects of opening up to one's parents about this potentially explosive subject, most authors urge serious deliberation, and perhaps continued silence, at least until the youth has established his own residence and formed viable emotional and financial ties outside the family.

Still, some sons foresee no obvious danger in coming out to their parents, yet remain unable to do so; ambivalence and uncertainty block their paths. Such an impasse is illustrated by the experience of Colby, a geology student at Southern Illinois University:

> I spent most of the summer of my sophomore year torn up inside about whether I should tell my mom and dad I was gay. I was living at home that summer and they kept asking me why I wasn't dating any girls. I made up all kinds of excuses. I felt like such a liar. . . . I thought, "If I tell them I'm gay, they'll freak." So I didn't tell them. So then I felt guilty about not telling them and leading them on. It was a terrible summer, a terrible time in my life. I was glad to go back to school. . . . The thing is, I really thought they would understand. It would take them a while, but they would understand. But I just couldn't do it right then.

Ultimately, a son caught in such a quandary must determine the extent to which being frank with his mother and father is essential to his happiness and to the enjoyment of his relationships with them. Some sons cannot or will not mislead their parents for any length of time while others believe that being truthful would probably prove disastrous for all concerned. Again, the decision is an individual one based on the son's values, his expectations of his parents' reactions, and his predictions of the long-term consequences.

Which brings us to a third issue: parental reactions. One writer has summed it up quite well with the simple observation that "parental reactions are not predictable."[5] Indeed, it is often very difficult to anticipate precisely how others will take the news. Yet a handful of studies have shed some light on the subject.

Researchers Linda Weinberger and Jim Millham, for instance, have found that a person who holds to the notion of separate roles for the two genders is more likely than others to reject a gay person.[6] This type of individual thinks in terms of clearly defined categories of human behavior ("a man should act like a man, a woman should act like a woman"), and therefore has difficulty adjusting to anything novel or unconventional, anything that does not fit into a traditional category. As could be expected, this includes homosexuality since, on the surface, this orientation appears to cross several established boundaries.

By comparison, the son whose parents are more liberal, resilient, and flexible in their thinking may have a different experience. Since his father and mother are less inclined to pigeon-hole others, they may adapt more readily to his same-sex nature.

A related factor is age. By and large, elderly parents tend to be more rejecting of a gay son, because such parents grew up at a time when fixed ideas about sexuality were common, when acceptable behavior for the two genders was more strictly defined.[7] As we have noted, Western society has historically confused homosexuality with sickness or sin, with the predictable result being that millions of people in more conservative times grew up with these views. Today, many of these same people are now parents, and they remain unable to discard, replace, or transcend such long-held misconceptions, even when it comes to their own children.

The son whose parents are younger, on the other hand, may have a better experience. He may find greater acceptance because his father and mother grew up in an era marked by an enhanced respect for individual differences, as well as a better understanding of the nature of human sexuality.

Still other research has focused on the quality of a son's relationship with his parents. If their relationship is already rocky, the disclosure may ignite a fiery reaction; the conditions are already in place for a negative outcome.[8] If, however, the parent and son share a strong and healthy bond, an attachment characterized by mutual respect and unhindered communication, the chances of a productive outcome may be greater. Particularly if they have gotten on well in the past and have discussed sensitive personal matters as they have emerged, the revelation of the son's homosexuality may be accepted more easily.

Again, though, we must remember that even in the best of circumstances—when parents are young, liberal, and generally supportive—they may still have reactions that seem entirely out of character for them. And negative emotional responses are the norm. They just vary in form, intensity, and duration.

Stages of Parental Adjustment

To better understand parental responses, Dr. Bryan Robinson at the University of North Carolina and Drs. Lynda Walters and Patsy Skeen at the University of Georgia studied 402 mothers and fathers of gay children.[9] The parents were contacted through two national support organizations, the Federation of Parents and Friends of Lesbians and Gays (PFLAG) and the National Federation of Parents and Friends of Gays (PFOG). The majority of the participants were well-educated, Caucasian mothers in their fifties, with most having middle- to upper-level incomes and describing themselves as "somewhat liberal."[10]

Parents who join such organizations do so in order to adjust to their children's sexual orientations and to help other parents do the same. We could assume, then, that a mother or father who feels wrenching antagonism toward homosexuality might be disinclined to join a PFLAG or PFOG group; the person might consider a negative reaction to be reasonable and appropriate and therefore something that does not need to be changed. Accordingly, the results from the following studies may perhaps represent a somewhat exceptional group of parents; namely, those who are concerned enough about their gay children, as well as their relationships with them, to join an organization solely to work on ensuring that the family remains intact and its network of relationships, healthy and fulfilling.

The Robinson Study

In their research, Dr. Robinson and his colleagues found that 64 percent of the parents in the support groups passed through a five-stage adjustment process. The stages themselves, in their order of appearance, consisted of shock, denial, guilt, anger, and acceptance.

Shock

Thirty-seven percent of the parents described being stunned upon learning that their children were gay, with many adding that they suddenly saw their children as strangers—as a "member of another species," as another researcher once put it;[11] this despite the fact that many of these same mothers and fathers had already wondered privately whether their children might be homosexual. Having their suspicions confirmed, however, was a startling experience. Among the parents' concerns was the worry that their sons might want to have sex-change surgery or that their other children might also be gay. Thus jolted by the news of their sons' sexual dispositions, the parents' concerns occasionally sailed beyond realistic bounds.

Denial

Most parents next described a period during which they refused to believe that their children were truly homosexual, clinging instead to the unlikely prospect that sooner or later their children would convert to heterosexuality. Sometimes this refusal to face reality took the form of a belief that a gay son was simply "going through a phase" and would eventually develop heterosexual interests. At other times, parents clung to the hope that he might someday meet the "right woman" and fall in love.

Guilt

Gradually, as the need to deny reality began to recede, remorse swept over the parents. Nearly two-thirds were saddened upon finally realizing that their children were indeed gay, with guilt being prominent in many cases, especially among the mothers. "I thought it was an illness caused by something I had done wrong or failed to do that I should have done," explained one mother.[12] Added a father, "I felt that early prejudices and remarks were coming back to haunt me—that it was payback time."[13] Nevertheless, most parents, in due time, stopped blaming themselves. In fact, nearly nine out of ten concluded that their child's sexual disposition was present at birth.

Anger

The next step in the adjustment process was marked by hostility, an emotion reported by 22 percent of the group. Of those parents who were angry, most were perturbed simply because their children were homosexual, although 4 percent were irritated because their children had chosen to tell them about it. Others were annoyed because their children had *not* told them earlier. "I was angry because my child didn't tell me sooner," said one parent.[14] "I felt he didn't trust me enough to know I wouldn't reject him. I didn't understand his fears and trauma about coming out." Still, of all the reactions that a mother or father could have, it is surprising that such a relatively small number reported hostility. We must remember, though, that this collection of individuals may have been unusual in that they may have been more reflective and tolerant than other types of parents.

Acceptance

Finally, after a period of information gathering and soul searching, the majority of parents arrived at a state of acceptance. "I was relieved to at last really know my son," said a seventy-two-year-old woman.[15] "At last he would be his true self. The invisible wall had finally disappeared. No more living two different lives—one for himself and one for the family he loves." Thus, most parents achieved a state of understanding whereby they could embrace their sons, accepting their sons' affinity for other men as a unique personal characteristic.

The DeVine Study

Another perspective on the adjustment process has been proposed by researcher Jack DeVine, who outlined a five-stage process of parental reconciliation to the news.[16] The first stage Dr. DeVine refers to as *subliminal awareness*—the pre-coming-out period when parents suspect that their son is gay, but do not know for certain that this is the case. Such conjecture may emerge because the son drops hints about his affectional and sexual interests or because his actions suggest that he may be gay. Thus, while the parents and child do not actually discuss the possibility of his being homosexual, because of their vague awareness of his sexual disposition they may not be caught completely off guard when he does eventually open up to them.

The second stage Dr. DeVine calls *impact*—the family crisis that ensues when a son tells his parents that he is homosexual or when they find out in some other fashion. At such a moment, the family is thrown into a state of chaos, with the parents experiencing any number of painful emotions. It is the dread of precisely this sort of ordeal, incidentally, that prompts some gay sons to decide against opening up to their families.

"I was shocked," said a mother recalling her reaction. "I didn't know what to say when he told me, but I was afraid he would tell his father and I knew it would just kill him. For days, I couldn't think of anything else but that my son was gay. My only son." This woman's description of her initial reaction is fairly typical of this period in the adjustment process.

The third stage, *adjustment*, occurs when the parents, having now moved beyond disbelief and disorganization, appeal to their son to change. Either they try to persuade him to become heterosexual or implore him to keep hidden his sexual orientation. Their primary concern, at this juncture, may be preserving the family's reputation in the community rather than recognizing and respecting their son's sexual and affectional needs.

The fourth stage, *resolution*, is the period during which the mother and father step back, reflect on the situation, and begin to realize that their understanding—or misunderstanding—of same-sex love does not apply to their son or, for that matter, to other gay people; that the myths and stereotypes that they have long held about gays and lesbians are simply wrong. As a result, they begin to redefine their understanding of homosexuality so that it becomes more accurate and their son more acceptable to them.

Also during this stage, they may grieve over the loss of their image of, and their hopes for, their "straight son." Having, until now, thought of him in basically heterosexual terms, the parents must now relinquish their false image of him, ushering in a period of mourning.

The fifth and final stage Dr. DeVine refers to as *integration*—the point at which the parents modify the son's role in the family so that he continues to play an active part in family affairs, but as an openly gay member rather than as a heterosexual impostor. It is now that they accept the fact that his sexual orientation is different from their own and create positive new ways of interacting with him, ways that neither shy away from nor reject his gayness; for instance, by welcoming his male partner into the family and regarding them, together, as a valued couple. Thus, the adjustment process is largely complete by this point, with the parents being at peace with their son and with his sexual disposition. And this characterizes the healthy adjustment, the one that benefits everyone concerned.

"I'm so proud of my son," said one mother of her gay child. "To do what he has done takes real courage. We all admire him so much."

Still, such positive comments notwithstanding, we should note that many parents never attain a point of healthy acceptance. They reach an impasse at an earlier stage and remain there indefinitely. Which brings us to those mothers and fathers who cannot seem to adjust completely to their sons' sexual dispositions, including those who are so disdainful of homosexuality that they permanently reject their children. And sadly, such ordeals do occur in some families.

Drs. Emery Hetrick and A. Damien Martin of the Institute for the Protection of Lesbian and Gay Youth now the Hetrick Martin Institute in New York City have much to tell us in this regard. These investigators looked at the difficulties reported by 329 gay adolescents seeking help from their facility, an agency that provides social and psychological assistance to gay adolescents.[17] Since their services include emergency placement, among other things, this was, by definition, a troubled group of youths.

Among the problems described by their young gay clientele, feelings of emotional and social isolation were the most frequent complaints, with worries about family relationships coming in second as the most commonly cited concern. A large number said that their families had rejected them for coming out, with 17 percent of the total group having been physically assaulted for this reason. Some had been kicked out of their homes as well and were thus seeking shelter. As for the possibility that these youths somehow failed to take notice of parental "danger signs" before telling their families, Drs. Hetrick and Martin found that, in some cases, there was no history of family problems prior to the disclosure of the sons' sexual orientations,[18] that the parents' reactions were wholly unexpected; a disconcerting finding, but one that is in accord with the observations of other researchers regarding the unpredictability of parental responses.

In light of these findings, Drs. Hetrick and Martin conclude that, at this young age level, coming out to parents is fraught with hazard:

> [W]e strongly recommend to clients who are still in high school that they think very carefully before coming out to their parents. We have seen several instances where a young person, confident of the love of his or her parent, reveals his or her homosexuality and then ends up on the street.[19]

And once he is on the street, anything can happen. Certainly, some youths, out of necessity, resort to the drug or sex trade to survive.[20] And this is not only disheartening in itself, but disturbing as well in that it places such youths at marked risk for further violence, as well as for serious disease. Indeed, it is estimated that the rate of HIV infection among homeless youths may reach as high as 12 percent in some cities. To be sure, loving parents do not hand over their children to such grim fates.

Recalls a gay adolescent who was thrown out of his home for telling his parents about himself:

> When I was thirteen, there was a boy in junior high with me whom I liked a lot. In fact, I was in love with him. My sexual

feeling for him scared me, but still that was how I felt. He was in an automobile accident, and for a while I thought he might die. I often cried because he meant so much to me. There was nothing sexual between us.

My mother noticed how unhappy I was and kept asking what was wrong. We had always been close so I finally got up the nerve to tell her that I was gay. She got upset and threw me out. She said she wasn't going to let me hurt my younger brother and sisters.

I didn't know what to do. I got some of my clothes and left. My dad was coming up the walk as I was leaving. He wasn't too upset. He just said, "You know how your mother is," and went inside.

I went to a massage parlor I had heard of and asked for a job. They were nice to me and even let me sleep there. I got the job, and I have been working there for five years now. I don't know what I would have done if they hadn't helped me out. I don't go to school anymore, but I'm making loads of money. I have more money than any kid my age that I know.

But I miss my family. Sometimes I walk up and down the street hoping my mom will let me in. Once she came out and told me that when the kids get bigger, I could visit, but so far I haven't been able to go in. Sometimes I go near where my dad works and see him when he goes out to lunch. He shakes my hand and says, "How's it going?" But he doesn't ask me to come home either. Someday maybe my parents will take me back. I keep hoping.[21]

Of course, when parents abandon a gay son merely because he does not share their heterosexual orientation, the whole issue of choice comes into focus. The fact is, the gay person has no real voice in being homosexual; as we have noted, in the large majority of cases his sexual orientation is a given. Choice enters into the picture only when he decides precisely *how* he is going to approach life as a gay person. And, of course, millions of homosexual youths and adults decide to accept and cultivate their same-sex dispositions, this being the healthiest response, although one that may be upsetting to certain types of family members. Still, this is no reason for their families to ostracize them. But at issue here is not what is fair, but what is fact. And there definitely are those families that discard forever their gay children, miscasting the biopsychosocial fact of sexual disposition as a moral issue, then passing judgment on it. And the irony is striking: by choosing to engage in a moral appraisal of what is essentially a nonmoral matter, then forsaking their child as a result, it is the parents who commit the truly malignant deed.

In my own professional experience, I have, from time to time, encountered gay youths who were expelled from their homes merely because they came out to their parents, with some of these youths never returning to their families. Of those who did, however, there often seemed to be an enduring reluctance on the part of the sons to forgive their parents or to ever fully trust them again. In view of what these adolescents sometimes endured outside the home, such lasting apprehension is entirely understandable.

So we ask, "Why are some parents able to adjust quite well to their son's same-sex disposition while others have a much harder time of it?" Of paramount importance, it would appear, are the family's principles and values, in addition to those characteristics that we noted earlier, such as the parents' ages and the preexisting quality of the parent-child relationship.

In this regard, researchers have found that the parents' philosophy of family life and the degree of closeness they share with their children play critical roles in their ability, and their willingness, to accept their gay sons. Those mothers and fathers who believe that unwavering affection is the mortar of the family unit may be much more likely to put forth the effort required to overcome their own resistance and embrace their sons than are those who are not as close to their children and who place a lower premium on family bonds.[22]

Another factor is the degree to which the father and mother are status-oriented. Those parents who are intensely preoccupied with projecting a conventionally wholesome public image may place their own needs for public approval and prestige above the mental and spiritual needs of their sons. As a result, the parents become stuck in one of the middle stages of the adjustment process, goading their children to conceal their true selves in order to maintain the family's image in the community.

Parents may also become lodged in a midrange stage when they define acceptable behavior in highly rigid terms. For the most part, parents who are by nature unyielding may have difficulty grasping that their son's sexual orientation is a rightful alternative to their own, perceiving it instead as a defective mechanism in need of repair.[23] Thus, they pathologize it, treating it as a deformity of character rather than a variation of behavior. They may therefore insist that their child change his sexual disposition to meet familial and societal expectations, and may never budge from this hard-line and entirely untenable position.

Of course, parents who are extremely dependent on social custom may also reject their sons because they believe this is what they are supposed to do. Unaccustomed to thinking for themselves, they turn to conventional teachings for instruction, and based on their interpretations of these teachings, renounce their sons because they do not conform to the historical Western male image.

In this regard, religion is often a chief consideration.[24] Some parents interpret their religion as teaching that love, compassion, and understanding are among the most noble of human qualities, and they apply these attributes in their efforts to adjust to their son's sexual orientation. In such a case, their religion helps them accept their child.

Other parents, by comparison, are drawn to that side of their religion that condemns certain behaviors as unacceptable. Consequently, their religion, as they choose to practice it, stalls their adjustment, causing them to remain fixed at an earlier stage in which they implore their sons to change.

Still others become caught between what they consider to be their religion's denunciation of homosexuality and their own natural love for their child. Such parents, if they are Christian, are typically unaware that their religion, prior to the twelfth century, did not disapprove of homosexuality; that important figures in Christianity's formative days are now believed to have been homosexual, and that same-sex relationships between men were held in high esteem in some cases, according to Yale historian and biblical scholar John Boswell, among others.[25] And this makes sense, given the fundamental values of the Christian faith: a nonjudgmental attitude, a recognition of the sanctity of human relationships, a respect for those who are different, and the goal of a diverse, yet harmonious, human community.

But being unaware of this and other historical information, many contemporary parents, mired in conflict, continue to believe that they must either accept their gay sons and, in so doing, defy their religions or reject their sons and retain the love of God. Deeply confused, they do not know which way to turn. And this is sad as well as unnecessary. If these parents could understand the facts about the same-sex orientation—that it is a biological and perhaps socially determined way of relating to the world and not an epic moral failing—and if they were more aware of the historical underpinning of their chosen religions, they might be better able to reconcile their son's sexual dispositions with their own spiritual beliefs. But many parents remain in the dark in this respect, such that the whole issue of the same-sex orientation continues to be profoundly troubling to them. Thus, just as a gay son must typically struggle to acknowledge and accept his sexual orientation, so, too, must the parents of gay sons grapple with an array of deeply personal and, at times, perplexing issues as they come to terms with the situation. Yet, like their gay children, millions of parents do proceed to adjust quite well, and go on to enjoy very loving, fulfilling relationships with their sons and their sons' partners.

TELLING ONE'S WIFE

Turning now to a distinctive group of men—gay husbands—it has been estimated that 20 percent of homosexual men marry women at some time in their lives,[26] with two-thirds of these unions ending in divorce.[27] These figures are no small matter, representing, as they do, several million people. The question, then, is why such marriages take place in the first place.

As one might expect, a large number of women who marry homosexual men apparently do not know that these men are, in fact, homosexual. They are simply attracted to them and assume that they are straight. Some writers have even suggested that, in some cases, women may be drawn to gay men because of certain personality characteristics that these men supposedly possess, such as thoughtfulness, sensitivity, and emotional accessibility.[28] Other researchers, however, have proposed that it is the personality characteristics of the women themselves that cause them to select homosexual men.

A woman who is uncomfortable being sexually intimate, for instance, may feel reassured in the company of a man who places few such demands on her. She may even marry him because she feels safe in such a sexually nonthreatening relationship, perhaps not realizing, at least not consciously, that his affectional and erotic interests lie elsewhere.[29]

That said, it should be noted that little empirical evidence exists to support this notion. Instead, the idea appears to be based on a limited number of psychiatric case studies, studies that may not be representative of the larger population of wives of gay men. Thus, while we cannot dismiss entirely the possibility that at least some women seek out homosexual men as a result of their own feelings of personal inadequacy or sexual insecurity, it may well be that the majority of gay men's wives are emotionally well-adjusted and quite comfortable with sexual intimacy, and that they enter into their marriages for altogether healthy reasons. Obviously, further research is needed.

It is important to note, too, that the husband himself may not have fully realized that he is homosexual until after he has wed. To be sure, in some marriages it appears that both partners come face-to-face with the man's same-sex orientation only after several years of sharing a home and raising a family together. Nevertheless, there are indeed those men who know, or at least suspect, that they are homosexual prior to marriage, yet wed anyway for any number of reasons.

First and foremost, the gay man may marry because he genuinely loves the woman and perhaps wishes to start a family with her. Thus, he enters into the marriage in good faith, with every intention of ensuring that it is a happy, successful alliance.

In other instances, a man may be conscious of his sexual and affectional needs for other men, but unable to accept this aspect of himself. He weds in the hope that living in a more conventional arrangement will somehow cause his homosexual needs to be replaced by heterosexual ones.

Still other men explain that it is pressure from their families that causes them to marry; that they are expected to "take a wife" and have children so as to preserve the family reputation and perpetuate the family name. If they do not, they may be disowned and possibly disinherited.

Similarly, some wed because of professional pressure to do so. They claim that they are in career fields in which it is necessary that they appear heterosexual in order to advance and prosper. And it is true that many professions do indeed favor married males, viewing them as the only qualified bearers of traditional power and authority. In fact, even those occupations that do not insist that their members be married may expect them to be straight nonetheless, which, to many observers, is proven by marriage—a quaint, but enduring, notion. Accordingly, some highly ambitious gay men, rather than being forthright about their sexuality or choosing career fields in which they would be less vulnerable to discrimination, decide to misrepresent themselves as heterosexual so that they might attain a measure of success in their preferred areas, even when this requires matrimony. And the list of reasons goes on and on.

As for why these men subsequently conceal their sexual orientations from their wives, most fear that the truth would wreck their spouses, while others worry that it would jeopardize their own standing in the community or workplace.[30] These may be valid concerns. After being in a marriage and establishing a reputation as a heterosexual, the revelation of the husband's homosexuality may well shock, disillusion, and confound his wife, as well as his friends and colleagues if they find out, which they very often do. Predictably, sometimes after coming out at home, a man will find himself suffering negative repercussions on the job or in the community because others have now learned that he is homosexual and that he presumably misled his wife.

In other cases, a husband may guard his sexual orientation because he believes that he may file for divorce at some point, and, if so, would probably seek sole or joint custody of the children. He believes that being gay could work against his efforts in such a circumstance. And he may well be right.

"It has been consistently reported that if a parent's homosexuality is raised as a custody issue," says researcher Eric Strommen, it "not only becomes the central issue in the custody case, but it makes a ruling in favor of the gay parent significantly less likely."[31] Frequently, gay fathers are denied custody of their children, with the court's justification nearly always based on unsupported assumptions. Like many private citizens, some judges still cling to antiquated myths when dealing with gay issues, often basing crucial judgments on unsubstantiated, even long disproven, notions. For the legally mindful gay man, then, his wish to come out to his wife may be overshadowed by his determination to stay in regular contact with their children.

The Decision to Disclose

In contrast to the man who chooses to remain closeted is the one who decides to open up to his spouse. In one study, researchers looked at two groups of husbands, those who knew prior to marriage that they were gay and who had already had sexual experiences with other men, and those who did not know that they were homosexual until after they were married.[32] The findings indicated that the men in the first group tended to gradually lose interest in their wives and drift back into same-sex relationships, while those in the second group were usually surprised, perplexed, and disturbed by the emergence of their same-sex desires. Driven by inner discord, the latter were more likely to inform their wives of these newly discovered urges so that together they could figure out a way of dealing with them.

Other studies have shown that a husband may come out to his wife not because he feels emotionally torn and in need of her help but simply because he wishes to be honest with her. This is frequently the case in those relationships that place great value on unfettered communication, unions in which the partners share the belief that most marital difficulties are surmountable if they are brought out into the light and discussed. As the husband sees it, his attraction to his own gender clearly constitutes one such difficulty.

A man may also come out to his wife in an effort to explain why they are experiencing problems in their marriage. Occasionally, this happens when the husband's thoughts, feelings, and fantasies are probed by a therapist in the course of marital therapy aimed at pinpointing the source of the couple's difficulties. As for the nature of the marital problems themselves, often they center around the couples' feelings of stagnation or frustration in the marriage. Other issues may involve the man's flagging sexual interest in his wife—a problem that may be inappropriately diagnosed as "impotence" or "erectile dysfunction"—or his increasing argumentativeness, bouts of depression, or unexplained absences from home that may occur when he explores the gay community or simply puts off going home to his wife. Only by facing the facts can such issues be resolved.

Of course, a husband may also fear that his wife is about to discover that he is gay and for this reason comes out to her; he prefers to have control over the manner in which she learns about it. In some instances, this may be an unrealistic worry; the man may simply feel guilty about his same-sex desires and therefore expects to be caught momentarily. In other instances, however, his concerns may be more realistic. If he is a member of a highly visible, influential, and conservative profession, for instance, there may be those who are aware of his sexual orientation and who could use this information against him. Or the man may be spending large amounts of time in the gay community where his presence could be easily spotted and conveyed to his wife. Or his wife may have recently come across some "evidence" of his homosexuality, such as a gay magazine in his car, the result being that he fears that sooner or later she will uncover more definitive proof. Rather than endure the gnawing dread of imminent discovery, he decides to tell her about this aspect of himself.

As for those instances in which the husband is further along in the coming-out process, he may be well past merely exploring the gay world and instead be involved in a long-term relationship with another man. He may even be planning to leave the marriage to be with this other person. For this reason, the man comes out to his wife. In the straight world, the entry of a new love interest is one reason why some marriages dissolve, and so it may be when one of the partners is gay.

In still other cases, the revelation occurs because changes in the family structure, or the prospect of such changes, make it necessary. A woman wishes to become pregnant, for instance, but her husband suspects that he may someday exit the relationship to pursue a life that is more compatible with his sexual disposition. Realizing that he would be making a parental commitment that he might not be present to honor, he tells his wife that he prefers not to have the child, and, just as important, he tells her why.

In much the same vein, a husband, aware that he is homosexual, may decide to keep this fact to himself until he fulfills his primary responsibilities as a father. Once his children reach adulthood and leave home, he comes out.

And finally, a gay husband may become HIV-infected and, for this reason, tell his spouse about his sexual orientation. In such a case, the disclosure of his homosexuality may be especially difficult for the woman to handle because it occurs within the context of some rather alarming medical news. And further worsening the matter may be the fact that she has had little or no time to brace herself for such a startling turn of events; the announcement comes without sufficient warning. In such a circumstance, she may feel truly devastated.

The Reactions of Wives

Even in the most favorable circumstances, the wife of a gay man is in a tough position. Unlike his parents, who may not be pleased to learn that their son is homosexual but for whom the information may otherwise have few, if any, immediate consequences, his wife must not only cope with the knowledge of his homosexuality, but must also grapple with the fact that the man has perhaps been unfaithful to her and may be planning to leave the marriage. Thus, there may be sexual, legal, and financial matters to consider, as well as issues pertaining to their children.

In terms of the timeline for her adjustment, it has been estimated that it takes at least one year for a woman to cope with the practical problems stemming from her husband's disclosure, two or more years to resolve the more complicated issues, and three or more years to get past the ordeal and build a new life for herself.[33] Of all the people to whom a gay man comes out, then, the news may have the greatest impact on, and the most far-reaching implications for, his spouse.

Stages of the Adjustment Process

As for the woman's reaction, like that of a gay man's parents, it often depends on the preexisting quality of their relationship, the reason for the disclosure, and the woman's familiarity with, and understanding of, homosexuality and the coming-out process. Despite individual and situational nuances, however, wives do tend to respond in similar ways.

In this regard, the adjustment process through which many women appear to pass may be conceptualized as consisting of a five-stage sequence, with the stages including (1) panic, isolation, and confusion, (2) loss and despair, (3) anger, (4) attempts to understand, and (5) reconciliation and the recovery of trust. Of course, due to the number and complexity of the issues involved, the sequence of these stages may not always occur in the order listed here. For instance, a woman may vacillate between anger and understanding, occasionally falling back into feelings of sadness and loss, yet all the while progressing toward reconciliation. Certainly, this is a perplexing time for most women, a time when they may feel that they have nothing solid to believe in or hold on to, including their husbands, since the men themselves may now be struggling to navigate their own turbulent waters.

Panic, Isolation, and Confusion

As for the first stage, upon learning that her husband is gay, a woman may be floored by the news and find it difficult to believe. Soon, however, she recovers from this state and may find herself feeling alone, confused, and beset with questions. She may wonder, for instance, how long her husband has known that he is gay and whether their marriage has been an illusion from the beginning. She may also wonder if he has been sexually active—perhaps unsafely so—with other men, and thus, whether he is HIV-infected; as well, she may worry that she herself may be infected. Lastly, she may be concerned, in more general terms, about the future of the family itself.

Unfortunately, during this time the woman may feel uncomfortable talking to her husband about these worries, either because she now mistrusts him or because she realizes that he is submerged in his own inner struggles and is therefore unable to offer any real help. She may also be reluctant to discuss the matter with friends or family, due to feelings of embarrassment, or because she fears that revealing her husband's sexual orientation might have negative repercussions for the family itself. In some instances, a husband will specifically ask that his wife not tell anyone for the moment. Thus, the woman may feel painfully alone, trapped in a relationship that is not what she thought it was, yet unsure where to turn or what to do next.

Of course, out of sheer panic, she may simply take their children and leave, at least for awhile. This may be due, in part, to the feeling that her husband is a stranger, an alien, and therefore someone with whom she wants no contact. Or it may be a way of escaping, bodily, from the overwhelming situation itself. During this time, the woman may also contact a lawyer and initiate divorce proceedings—yet another way of erecting a wall between herself and her husband. These seemingly impulsive actions are not uncommon. At this step in the adjustment process, the woman is functioning in a crisis mode, unsure of her husband, unsure of herself, and perhaps uncertain of the nature of reality itself. Her customary way of understanding the world thrown into doubt, she may no longer trust her own perceptions. By taking such action, then, she distances herself from the source of stress—her husband and the situation in the home—while regaining at least a limited sense of control over the matter.

Loss and Despair

Next, as the feeling of alarm begins to ebb, the woman may find herself experiencing remorse and guilt, and may begin blaming herself, at least in part, for the situation. And while this reaction may seem somewhat puzzling, it is nevertheless true in many cases. Sometimes this is because the woman loves her husband very deeply and does not want to think badly of him; she would rather think badly of herself. At other times, it is related to the fact that women in our society have traditionally been conditioned to view themselves as the responsible party in family matters, such that whenever a serious predicament occurs in her family, regardless of its actual cause, the woman may be prone to attribute it to herself.

"At first I decided I hadn't been a good enough wife," said Kathleen, a wife who experienced such a reaction. "I decided that I must be missing something, that there was this lack in me that made Ron turn to other men. It took me a long time to get over that feeling."

Another reason for self-blame may be because the husband, wishing to avoid sexual intimacy with her, routinely criticizes his wife's sexual needs over the years. He spurns her advances for physical closeness by implying that there is something wrong with her need for affection, causing her to feel physically and emotionally undesirable. Accordingly, when the woman eventually learns that her husband is homosexual, she may take this fact as confirmation that her suspicions about herself are true; that had she somehow been a better or more attractive woman, he would not have "turned queer" on her. To be sure, learning that a husband is gay can injure a woman's sexual self-image. And yet some wives experience the opposite reaction: they are, in one sense, genuinely relieved to discover that their husbands are attracted to other men, since they now realize that, as women, they are not to blame for the men's lack of interest in them.

Besides struggling with feelings of self-blame, a wife usually experiences a strong sense of loss as well, accompanied by feelings of sadness, depression, and despair. This is because, in a very real sense, she *has* lost her husband, or at least her long-held image of him, as well as her marriage or, perhaps, her previous way of knowing it. And if divorce is the eventual outcome—and statistics indicate that it usually is—she may have lost the feeling of security and stability that she found in the structure of her marriage, in the easy comfort of its day-to-day routines. Most disturbing of all, though, the woman may have lost her faith in reality itself, experiencing in its place a disquieting sense of free-fall.

Anger

As could be expected, hostility may enter the picture at this point. Although some women become enraged immediately upon finding out that their partners are gay, many experience their most intense anger later on, after they have worked through other emotions. The strength of this hostility can be striking, as evidenced by the following account from one wife:

> My deep rage persists to this day, five years later. Anger is my only connection to Tim's gayness, though he's never felt it directly. . . . Someday if the occasion arises, he'll receive my wrath. When he does, the issue won't be the Catholic Church's homophobia, which made him do what he did. The issue will be what he did to me—not asking me, not telling me before we married, not giving me a choice.[34]

As this passage illustrates, a wife may feel that her husband knowingly betrayed her, igniting a firestorm of anger. She may believe that he knew before they wed that he was gay and that he married her anyway, either to use her as a false front or perhaps as a vessel for producing children. In reality, as we have noted, it may well be that the husband did not know that he was gay prior to the marriage. This is often the case. Yet even if he did have his suspicions, this in no way implies that he married in order to exploit the woman. Nevertheless, her trust shaken, a wife may find herself feeling duped, the result being a sense of violation, suspiciousness, and rage.

Accordingly, she may lose all faith in her husband. Believing that he intentionally misled her about his sexual orientation in the past, the woman may now question most anything he says in the present. For instance, if he claims that he has had sexual fantasies about other men but has never acted on them, or perhaps that he has had only one or two male sexual partners during his entire adult life, she may assume that he is not being truthful; she may believe that he has had erotic encounters with a parade of male lovers.

Other reasons for hostility stem from the multiple losses the wife typically incurs. When the woman feels that her world has fallen apart because her husband is homosexual, when she no longer feels that she knows him, and when their life together feels unreal and counterfeit, she may blame him for bringing about such a painful situation. She may feel that he has destroyed their family and permanently damaged their children's futures. "How could you do this to us?" a wife will ask. "How could you do this to our children?" Enraged and indignant, she does not yet grasp that her husband's sexual orientation is not a choice, not a moral act for which he must be held accountable. The fact is, the woman in deep pain and is responding as a spurned lover and a protective mother.

Of course, a wife may feel offended, too, because her husband did not tell her sooner that he is gay, a delay which she may interpret as an indication that he did not trust her. At this point in the adjustment process, she may not yet realize that it may have taken the man, himself, several years to recognize that he is homosexual; moreover, that the discovery itself may have been very recent and that he confided in her as soon as he was certain of it. Thus, because she does not understand the coming-out process, the woman may not appreciate the pain, isolation, and guilt that her husband most likely suffered before telling her about himself, nor realize the trust, as well as the courage, that it took for him to finally come out to her. Instead, she feels angry at him for supposedly being dishonest and, perhaps, critical of herself for presumably being thought of as untrustworthy.

Regardless of the causes of her anger, from this sense of rage a woman may seek to avenge herself. In some cases, she uses the man's same-sex orientation as a way to battle him in court for custody of their children. In other cases, she uses it to undermine his reputation in the community or the workplace. It appears, however, that most wives do not react in such ways, at least not for long periods of time. Either the woman realizes that such vindictive actions may backfire, harming not only her husband but also herself and their children, or she successfully vents her anger and comes to view the situation more objectively. She may set out to learn more about homosexuality itself, if she has not done so already, partly as a way of gaining a feeling of mastery over the situation. And this makes sense. As long as homosexuality remains a phantom in her life, an intruder into her marriage and family, it will continue to be a formidable threat, an ever-present danger. By peeling away its mystery, however, the woman may become better able to manage it. And this brings us to the fourth stage of the adjustment process.

Attempts to Understand

Eventually, the wife of a gay man usually finds herself wanting to know the facts about the same-sex disposition. In fact, this may now be an urgent need. At first, when she is perhaps somewhat embarrassed by the subject, she may seek information only from books. As the woman becomes more comfortable with the topic, however, she may seek out gay people in the community for discussion or may join a support group for spouses of gay people. And as she becomes more knowledgeable about the subject, a wife usually becomes more accepting of her husband and notices improvements in her own self-esteem as well. This may be, in part, because she is now less likely to blame herself, consciously or unconsciously, for her husband's sexual disposition. Like the concerned parents of a gay son who seek to learn about the same-sex orientation so they may better know their child, the wife who makes it a point to learn about homosexuality tends to adjust more quickly and satisfactorily to the situation.

Reconciliation and the Recovery of Trust

At last, having waded through her feelings of sadness and loss, discharged her anger, and acquired factual knowledge, the woman may find herself more reconciled to the situation. She may also begin to trust again, if not her husband, at least others in her life and in life itself. This is a crucial gain; the reestablishment of trust is instrumental in her adjustment.

The woman may also begin to see herself in a new and different light, as a stronger, more resilient person, and may feel more empowered as a result. And while feelings of unsteadiness may persist in certain respects—for instance, doubts about her attractiveness and desirability as a woman may continue to trouble her—she may nevertheless find herself enjoying greater self-confidence and a stronger sense of authority in, and control over, her life.

Of course, as a more decisive person, the woman may now decide to divorce her husband, if she has not arrived at this solution already. As it stands, most wives in this situation come to realize that their marriages, even under the best of circumstances, will probably not be sufficiently fulfilling to either partner over the years, and that divorce is the most reasonable course of action. One woman described her decision this way:

> I knew we should get a divorce. Our marriage just wasn't working. It hadn't worked for a long time, and now I could see

that it never would. Divorce was the only answer that made any sense. But it wasn't an easy thing to do. I was worried about what we would tell the kids. I didn't want them to be mad at their dad. . . . and I figured there would be all kinds of questions from our friends, and there were, too . . . For awhile we didn't tell anyone why we were doing it. We just weren't ready for that, so we said all the usual things. We gave all the usual answers. Now I think just about everybody knows, but then it's been over four years.

Like his wife, the husband may also recognize the necessity of a divorce, but this does not mean that he relishes the prospect of separating from his wife and children. In fact, he may dread it immensely.

"Even though the man may want to dissolve the marriage because he cannot achieve full life satisfaction within its heterosexual framework, he often feels torn," says Frederick Bozett of the University of Oklahoma Health Sciences Center.[35] "He has loved his wife, he may still love her, and he loves his children. He cherishes both the history he had developed with his family and the material possessions they have accumulated over time. To alter the security of a known relationship for an unknown and unpredictable future is difficult, especially if it involves leaving the children." Yet the husband usually proceeds with the divorce either because he feels it is the best course of action or because his wife insists on it.

In the most successful cases, when divorce is the outcome the woman goes on to build a meaningful life for herself, but with significantly less animosity toward her ex-husband and his sexual disposition. Likewise, the husband creates for himself a healthy, gratifying life as an openly gay man.

It should be noted, though, that some women decide to stay in their marriages, including those who are so emotionally dependent on their husbands that they cannot let go of them,[36] as well as those whose religions forbid divorce or who believe that they must remain together for the benefit of the children. In such cases, the couple, if they have not already done so, usually restructures their relationship around emotions and interests other than those that are romantic in nature. As for sexual gratification, some couples allow for the wife and husband to develop intimate relationships outside the marriage while a smaller number bring another man into the marital relationship itself.

TELLING ONE'S CHILDREN

The last group of family members to be considered in this chapter, and one that may play a crucial role in a man's decision to come out, is his children. Research suggests that nearly half of the marriages between gay men and straight women produce sons and daughters,[37] meaning that perhaps as many as 10 percent of homosexual men are fathers.[38] It has been further estimated that well over three million children in the United States have gay or bisexual parents.[39] While some fathers do disclose their same-sex orientations to their children, usually when they are in their teens or beyond,[40] most decide not to come out, for myriad reasons.

For many men, the most pressing concern is that the disclosure might upset or confuse their children, possibly causing the children to feel stigmatized and ashamed, their self-esteem plummeting in the process. And yet, there appears to be little chance of such harm occurring if the child is emotionally well-balanced prior to the disclosure. While some sons and daughters do become dismayed upon finding out that their fathers are gay, lasting emotional scars appear to be the exception. Nevertheless, there are those counselors who recommend that gay men not tell their children, opinions that may arise from the counselors' own unresolved sexual conflicts or fears of homosexuality, as well as their unfamiliarity with the facts about the effects of parental sexuality on child development.

"Typically, when the issue is raised in therapy many therapists advise against coming out to the children," says Dr. Edward Dunne, Adjunct Professor of Psychiatry at the College of Physicians and Surgeons, Columbia University, "but little evidence exists to support the suggestions of dire consequences to the children provided the father is able to remain in a close enough relationship with his children to foster understanding and acceptance."[41]

Fathers may worry, too, that the disclosure will change forever the parent-child relationship. They fear that their sons or daughters will become disrespectful of them, if not blatantly rebellious, and therefore harder to manage in the home. Or they worry that as parents they will become overly indulgent after the revelation, this creating problems in itself. Some also fear that their children will blame them if a divorce results from the homosexual issue and that this will diminish their effectiveness as parents.

In reality, however, formal research has uncovered few differences between the parenting experiences of straight and openly gay fathers. Researchers Jerry Bigner and R. Brooke Jacobsen at Colorado State University compared twenty-four homosexual fathers with twenty-nine heterosexual fathers and found that there were "almost no differences . . . (in terms of) degree of involvement with children's activities, degree of intimacy with children, problem solving, provision of recreation for children, encouragement of their autonomy, and the manner in which problems of child-rearing are handled."[42] And this has been the conclusion of other investigations as well.

Still, a few studies have found minor—and positive—differences. One study, for instance, reported that openly gay, divorced fathers are especially decisive as parents, are less inclined to use corporal punishment on their children, make deliberate attempts to rear their children in ways that foster an understanding of those who are different, and encourage fairness in attitudes.[43]

The available research, then, would appear to support the notion that coming forward as gay does not render a man less efficient as a parent. In fact, in certain cases, it may even increase his effectiveness.

As for a father's fear that he will be blamed for the divorce, many children do not hold him responsible if the family unit dissolves as a result of his disclosure. The truth is, many children are relieved to discover that their parents' separation is due to issues involving only the parents themselves and are less inclined to blame themselves for the ensuing changes in the family structure.[44]

Of course, some gay fathers do not come out to their children because of custody concerns or because their wives have forbidden it. In the latter case, the woman may feel that the matter should be kept between the spouses, that their children are not yet emotionally equipped to deal with the matter.

In other instances, a man may worry that if he comes forward, the disclosure might influence his children to become homosexual themselves when this might be contrary to their underlying heterosexual orientations. This is sometimes referred to, rather sardonically, as the "contamination theory" of homosexuality, the erroneous belief that merely knowing an openly gay person will somehow make one homosexual. In actuality, studies indicate that having a gay parent has little, if any, impact on a child's psychosexual development.[45] Just as heterosexual parents have homosexual sons and daughters, so too do homosexual parents have heterosexual ones.

"Concerns are typically expressed about the likelihood that children raised in gay families will become homosexuals themselves or that the gay parent will attempt to seduce the same-sex child," say researchers Robert Barret and Bryan Robinson.[46] "Research indicates that both of these myths are simply not supported in actual life. Children in gay families are as well-adjusted as all kids. . . . there is no indication that having a gay father is necessarily an impairment."

Lastly, some fathers fear that if they disclose their sexual orientations to their children, as well as to the community at large, their children may become vulnerable to harassment, a concern shared by many courts when making custody decisions.[47] Yet the likelihood of a child being subjected to this sort of persecution may not be as great as one might expect. As in so many other areas of gay parenthood, formal studies fail to support this assumption. Researcher Eric Strommen, reviewing the literature on the subject, concluded that harassment does not appear to be a problem for the majority of these children, perhaps in part because the children themselves are judicious in how they manage the information.[48]

In all, then, it appears that the reasons that fathers offer for concealing their same-sex orientations from their children are frequently based on faulty information—and probably on the fathers' own discomfort talking to their children about the issue—and, therefore, are largely unwarranted. Accordingly, upon realizing that this is the case, some men decide to broach the subject with their children.

The Decision to Disclose

In the best cases, the father is comfortable with his sexual orientation and, quite naturally, wishes to discuss it with those to whom he feels closest, including his children. He sees no reason to keep under wraps this constitutional part of himself. As well, he may wish to educate his children about the reality of the same-sex disposition, rather than having them be exposed to, and perhaps absorb and believe, any misinformation they may encounter outside the home. And his objective may be achieved: educating one's son or daughter in this way can effectively broaden the child's awareness of the spectrum of human diversity, as well as foster a respect and appreciation for the gay population in particular.

Other fathers, by comparison, may not yet feel entirely comfortable being both gay men and fathers, but believe that to be good parents they should be up front with their children whenever possible, especially in affairs of great importance. Feeling that it is hypocritical to teach their children to value honesty while at the same time misleading them in this particular matter, they feel a responsibility to open up to their children.

In a similar fashion, a father may come out because he is experiencing symptoms of HIV infection. He discusses the situation with his children so that they will have reliable information about his condition, its medical management, and its place in his life, rather than learning about it through perhaps less dependable and less thoughtful individuals in the community.

And then there is the individual who feels so awful about being both a gay man and a father—in his view, opposite ends of the spectrum of respectability—that he makes the announcement as a way of absolving his guilt and releasing unbearable tension. But this is a dubious reason for coming out to a son or daughter. While it may make the father feel better, the disclosure may be deeply troubling to the child. As it stands, a child is more able to accept a father's sexual orientation when the man has already come to terms with it himself and is visibly at ease being gay.[49] A conflicted father's guilt-ridden "confession" to his children is not the ideal way of presenting the facts to them.

In still other instances, a man explains his same-sex disposition to his children because he and his wife are planning to divorce, at least in part because of his sexual and affectional needs. By telling his children the real reason for the breakup, the man believes that they will be less inclined to hold themselves responsible for the impending changes in the family. That said, some children do subsequently blame the dissolution of the family, part and parcel, on the father's homosexuality—and, thus, on the father himself—even in cases in which the man's sexual orientation is not the principal reason for the divorce.

Finally, a father may have already separated from his wife and established an intimate relationship with another man, one with whom he is in the process of building a life and perhaps sharing a home. He tells his children about himself and his new partner so that they will understand the nature of his relationship with this gentleman to whom he has grown close.

The Reactions of Children

As for the way in which children tend to respond to the news, it depends, in large part, on the child's age, his or her concept of homosexuality,[50] the family's social background, the quality of the child's relationships with the parents, and any HIV-related fears the child may harbor. Nevertheless, it has been observed that, as a group, children tend to be more accepting of a gay father than are other groups of relatives. In fact, research reveals that gay fathers are often surprised by the favorable responses of their children.[51]

Age

Regarding age, studies indicate that children who are quite young are usually the most accepting,[52] in part because they may consider their father's sexuality to be irrelevant to their own lives; also, because they are largely unaware of the social stigma attached to male homosexuality. As for their future adjustment, since these children may remain in regular contact with their openly gay fathers, their fathers' sexual orientations becomes a routine part of their own lives. For this reason, as they grow older, such children usually continue to handle the matter well; they have become accustomed to, and comfortable with, the whole issue.

By comparison, older children, particularly those in their teens, may have more difficulty adjusting to the news. This may be because such youths, through contact with society, have already internalized negative stereotypes about the gay population and have thus learned to reject homosexual people out of hand. As well, they may be struggling with their own sexual and gender issues, a normal and predictable occurrence during this developmental period. Discovering that their fathers are gay, then, may in some cases add to their own turmoil and confusion. At such times, close parental guidance and emotional support may be very helpful, as well as professional assistance in more complicated cases.

As for the gay father's adult children, usually they have an easier time adjusting to the revelation. Typically, they have developed full lives for themselves, have created families of their own, and may live far away from the parents. Accordingly, their awareness of their father's disclosure tends to have less direct impact on their lives.

Social Background

Another factor that may affect a child's reaction is the family's social circle. A child in a conservative family, one that lives in a confined social world in which the members have contact with only those people who are very much like themselves, may never knowingly meet a gay person. As a result, the only information the child receives about such individuals may come from his parents or teachers and may be gravely distorted. Learning that his or her father is gay, then, may mean to the child that this man now falls into a category of people who are very different and unfamiliar, perhaps even alien and frightening, making the child's adjustment much more difficult.

In contrast, the son or daughter who grows up in a family with diverse social contacts, including friends, relatives, or neighbors who are gay, may find it easier to cope with the father's disclosure. Having already known and perhaps been quite fond of gay people, the child understands and accepts it in the father much more readily.

Reason for the Disclosure

Still another factor concerns the context of the disclosure itself. If a man comes out as part of a larger announcement that he and his wife are divorcing, then these prospective changes, in concert, may make the child's adjustment somewhat harder. Of the two pieces of information, however, it is believed that a child usually has more difficulty coping with the news of the divorce itself. Still, taken together, the two announcements may be overpowering. If, on the other hand, the father comes out at a time when the family situation is stable and reliable and its future more assured, the child may be better able to deal with the disclosure.

Relationship with the Father

Of course, a child's reaction may also be affected by his or her relationship with the father. If the two have gotten along well together in the past—if they have had a loving, trusting relationship—then the child may receive the disclosure more favorably. Since the child loves and perhaps admires the father, he or she may be inclined to accept this new information about him without reservation. By comparison, if the parent-child relationship is already marked by animosity, then the disclosure may simply serve as one more point of contention. In such a case, it may not be the father's sexuality to which the child truly objects; the gay issue may serve merely as fresh fodder for an ongoing struggle.

HIV-Related Concerns

Lastly, a child's fears related to HIV infection may be an important factor in his or her ability to cope with the disclosure. As it stands, some children become inordinately fearful that their fathers will contract the virus, become ill, and no longer be a vital part of the family. Thus, fears of abandonment may loom, especially if the child is also facing the prospect of the parents' separation or divorce.

At such times, the father, regardless of whether or not he is HIV-infected, may find it useful to discuss with his child the AIDS epidemic, while reassuring the child that, as a father, he will continue to be an active presence in the child's life, if this is indeed true. He may also find it helpful to offer accurate information about HIV illness, its prevention, and its medical management. In most such cases, a combination of emotional support and reliable information is sufficient in calming a child's anxieties.

Ultimately, the decision to come out to one's children should occur only after serious deliberation and planning. The father should understand thoroughly his reasons for coming out, should gauge the announcement so that, if possible, it occurs during a stable period in the child's life, and should tailor the disclosure to fit the child's age and level of understanding. If it is well-planned and properly executed, a disclosure of this type may yield several long-term benefits, among them a heightening of understanding and affection between members of the family, as well as a strengthening of the cohesiveness among the family members themselves. Says Callie, a thirteen-year-old girl:

> The good thing is that things are so open in my family. You don't have to hide anything from each other. Some fathers don't even tell their family they are gay. We have such a good relationship. I think knowing Dad is gay brings us closer together. . . . I talk about my dad all the time, but my friends never talk about theirs. When they do talk about them, I get the feeling that they're not as close to them.[53]

Certainly there are advantages and disadvantages of being forth-right with one's children about this matter, and it is the responsibility of each gay father to weigh the various factors and arrive at a decision about coming out. Of course, a substantial part of this decision may be based on the reactions of his wife and on the state of their marriage. In this regard, if the man has the support and cooperation of his spouse, including her actual participation in the disclosure process itself, the experience may be easier and more beneficial for all concerned.

As we have seen in this chapter, whether it is a man coming out to his wife and children or a son coming out to his mother and father, the revelation of one's homosexuality may test severely the love and integrity of the family unit itself. And while this is unfortunately the case, it is to be expected as long as our society persists in keeping male homosexuality an orientation shrouded in mystery and myth. But if the gay person's family is able to move beyond the stifling stereotypes, if it is able to pull together in affection and mutual respect, then its bonds may become stronger than ever before and the relationships between the gay individual and his loved ones deeper, more honest, and more truly authentic. To be sure, it is during such challenging moments that a family may discover within itself hidden wells of loyalty and honor and, in the process, the true meaning and purpose of the family itself.

SUGGESTIONS

The following suggestions are for the son who is considering coming out to his parents and the gay man who is contemplating telling his wife and possibly his children about his orientation. Recommendations are also offered to the parents and wives of these individuals.

1. If you are a son who is planning to come out to his parents, consider telling a trusted brother, sister, or other relative first, then enlisting that person's help in planning the announcement. Also, consider the advantages of coming out to one parent, then asking that person to assist you in telling the other one. Some people prefer to do it that way. In fact, studies show that gay sons occasionally choose to tell their mothers first, then later, their fathers.[54] The point is that you should review your options and select the method that seems to hold the greatest likelihood of a favorable outcome.

2. If you are an adolescent or a young adult and are emotionally and perhaps financially dependent on your mother and father, think about the consequences of a negative reaction on their part; namely, personal rejection and possibly eviction from your home. Knowing your parents as you do, if you feel that such a reaction is likely, reconsider telling them. It may be better to wait until you are in a position of greater emotional and financial independence.

If, however, you decide to go forward with the disclosure anyway, then at least develop a practical plan of action before doing so. Decide in advance who you will contact for emotional and financial support if outside help becomes necessary and where you will live if you are displaced. This may mean collecting the names of contact persons, phone numbers, and addresses of organizations in your local area and acquainting yourself with the services they offer, most notably emergency assistance. Do your homework so you will be ready to take action if complications should arise.

3. If you are a parent and your son tells you that he is gay, do not dismiss the statement as indicating that he is confused or "going through a stage." Not only may this conclusion be flatly wrong, but it may also insult your son by relegating his feelings and concerns to the level of triviality. As a consequence, he may thereafter refrain from discussing with you his sexual orientation, as well as other important personal matters.

Bear in mind, too, that his same-sex disposition was probably determined by forces largely beyond his, and your, control; forces that may have been in place as early as his conception. Accordingly, there is no need for you to introduce blame into the situation, either toward yourself or toward him.

Also, when he tells you, try not to overreact. Avoid verbally demeaning your child and do not physically harm him or expel him from the home. This is child abuse, and there is absolutely no justification for it. Rather, try to recognize and respect the fact that he gathered the courage to share with you this rather sensitive fact about himself, and strive to understand it. Take time to learn about homosexuality—what it is and what it isn't—all the while, conveying to your son that you love him and value him. And realize that you are not alone; many parents are confused and dismayed upon first receiving this news, but with time, knowledge, and above all, love, go on to enjoy fine relationships with their gay sons. To this end, joining a support group for the parents of gay children may be helpful.

4. If you are a married man and are considering coming out to your wife and perhaps your children, be aware that this will almost certainly change your family relationships, dramatically and irreversibly. And because it is such a consequential act, plan ahead to ensure that the announcement's long-range effects will be as beneficial as possible for all concerned.

A word of caution: if you have reason to believe that the disclosure will culminate in a divorce, as it often does, remember that custody decisions seldom favor gay fathers. Be aware, too, that you may receive hostile reactions from members of the extended family, particularly your former in-laws, if they discover that the divorce was due to the fact that you are gay. Plan ahead for such complications.

As for telling your son or daughter, the disclosure itself should be stated in terms befitting the child's age and level of intellectual and social development. Adapt the explanation to the child's capacity to understand. Going into too much detail, especially technical sexual detail, may be meaningless or even confusing or frightening to a youngster. Instead, a broad explanation about two people of the same gender caring about one another may be sufficient. For assistance in this regard, you might explore the various books that offer guidance to parents on the topic of sex education in general, as well as children's books aimed at educating them about homosexual relationships in particular, books like *Daddy's Roommate* and *How Would You Feel If Your Dad Was Gay?*[55] (publisher: Alyson Publications, Alyson Wonderland division).

And finally, be aware that millions of gay men are, or have been, both husbands and fathers, and that many of them have chosen to divulge their sexual orientations to their families. The result is that many of these men remain on good terms with their wives, or ex-wives, and their sons and daughters, indicating that it is entirely possible to resolve the situation in a healthy, satisfying fashion.

5. Lastly, if you are a woman and your husband tells you that he is gay, do not blame yourself for his sexual orientation. Being gay is not a sickness, a sin, or a crime; there is no reason for blame to be involved in the issue at all. Understand, too, that in all likelihood your husband was homosexual long before he ever met you, although he may not have known it when the two of you wed. Then try to adopt the most constructive approach possible to the situation.

You might, for instance, focus on the fact that he trusted and respected you enough to tell you this truth about himself; surely this was not an easy thing for him to do. As well, you might commit yourself to resolving with him this very human dilemma, knowing full well that the process may end in divorce. And if it does end in a legal dissolution, keep in mind that while a marriage to a gay man is typically fraught with problems, many couples who have weathered these tribulations have gone on to become close and good friends after the divorce, their marriages transformed into mature and lasting friendships. If you care deeply about your husband, this might be your goal as well.

Chapter 3

The Professional Sphere: Coming Out in the Workplace

Despite living in a democratic nation during an era of unprecedented emphasis on self-expression, the majority of gay men in the United States today conceal the fact that they are homosexual when they are on the job. A 1989 poll of the gay population, for instance, found that roughly 40 to 70 percent of the respondents had not disclosed their sexual orientations to those with whom they work.[1] Thus, while a substantial number of homosexual men are openly gay in their personal lives, when they are in their workplaces they remain largely closeted, at most coming out to a few other gay employees or perhaps to a handful of trusted heterosexual co-workers. And the millions of men who conceal their sexual dispositions in this context offer a litany of reasons for doing so, among them the belief that, in most fields, they are simply not welcome.

Of course, they are right. Historically in Western society, the workplace has not embraced, let alone actively recruited, homosexual men into its ranks. Rather, gay men have been expected to hide their orientations in order to secure and keep a job or to detour into a vocational area considered to be gay, meaning one that is innocuous to the public, a field having no real impact on society.

The mainstream population, for instance, has long accepted the presence of gay men in benign areas such as the fashion industry and interior design, two fields that usually do not touch directly on the lives of ordinary citizens in significant ways. It has not accepted them, however, in more consequential professions, like investment banking or politics. Viewed as dispensable outsiders in our society, gay men have likewise been regarded as ill-placed and expendable in the vocational world.

Furthermore, openly homosexual men, having been relegated to a narrow range of professions, have then been ridiculed in these occupational roles. Who among us has not been saturated with images of the histrionic hairdresser, the fussy interior decorator, and the mincing fashion designer? The enduring figure of the openly gay working man is that of a haughty, flamboyant, and fastidious creature, the image of a clown. Until recently, Western society was blind to the existence of millions of homosexual men in the halls of education, law, finance, athletics, mental health, medicine, and the military, among other areas; men who went undetected, in part, because they did not fit the farcical stereotypes. Of course, such men were also compelled by custom to exist in deep cover, meticulously hiding their orientations so that they might acquire, retain, and succeed at their jobs. Nearly always, the act of coming out meant exchanging careers and livelihoods for uncertain futures. All too often, it meant professional suicide.

In this chapter, we examine the issues that arise today when a man discloses his same-sex orientation in the workplace. We look at the professional lives of gay men in such areas as science, business and industry, and the military, with attention to the perils and profits of being *out* in these fields. But we begin by exploring that element of the gay male workforce that panics our society the most: those who hold jobs that entail close contact with children. As could be expected, mainstream society reacts with alarm to this group of professionals due to the persistent, though long-disproven, myth that homosexual men are potential pedophiles, as well as to the mistaken assumption that a child having long-term exposure to a gay man will grow up to be homosexual too, either through recruitment or through a social modeling process. As a result, men whose jobs involve direct contact with youths are among the most reluctant to divulge their same-sex orientations in the workplace, as we shall see in the first section of this chapter.

ELEMENTARY AND SECONDARY EDUCATION

Of those fields that require significant involvement with children, perhaps the most visible and influential is elementary and secondary education. It has been estimated that there are well over a quarter of a million gay teachers in the United States,[2] a substantial portion of whom find themselves in a bind.

In our society, the educational system through which children and adolescents must pass is an important instrument of social control, methodically indoctrinating youth in society's opinions, attitudes, and values in order to produce citizens who comply with conventional expectations. It should come as no surprise, then, that society expects its educators to be heterosexual, since this is the only orientation deemed acceptable by the mainstream population. But this particular requirement is inappropriate, as well as deeply problematic, for the man who wishes to be a teacher, yet who happens to be gay. It forces him to either misrepresent himself and thereby compromise his integrity or be honest about himself and suffer the consequences.

As it stands, some gay teachers fail to acknowledge the problem at all. They contend that their sexual dispositions are a private matter having no bearing on their teaching practices. They say that they are gay on their own time; that at work, they are in a professional, and therefore neutral, role. Many other gay teachers do not agree with this position, however, but do feel that the profession itself expects them to maintain such an artificial distinction. Indeed, research on the issue has shown that a significant portion of gay instructors believe that if they do not erect barriers between their professional and personal lives, they risk termination from their jobs.[3] And yet, when a teacher attempts to split off such a fundamental part of himself as his sexual orientation, he discards the very real fact of his unique personality, his lifelong experience as a member of a vilified minority, and his place in a social matrix that largely opposes his existence. Thus, whether or not he is aware of it, he may be depriving his students of valuable information, as well as a singular perspective on current political and social events. He also may be curtailing sharply the degree to which he is candid with them about the day-to-day aspects of his life, a healthy informality that is customary in many schools between heterosexual teachers and their pupils.

Of course, there *are* those gay educators who are very much aware of the conflict inherent in their circumstances and of the challenge it poses to their integrity and professional abilities. These are teachers who are disturbed by the clash between society's expectation that they be heterosexual and their own legitimate need to express themselves forthrightly in their work. They are aware, too, that being closeted may shortchange their students by withholding from them information that could expand their pupils' knowledge and enhance their lives.

Quite often, such teachers complain that they spend too much time dodging personal questions from their colleagues and skirting topics that could bring to light their same-sex orientations, time that they could better spend on job-related tasks. Besides side-stepping sensitive issues with their co-workers, however, they say that they also tend to avoid certain topics in the classroom for fear that a particular discussion might somehow lead to a revelation of their sexual dispositions. Obviously, in such cases, both the teacher and the student suffer. Heterosexual students, for instance, may be deprived of information that could help them recognize and correct any misunderstandings they might have about, and bigotry toward, minority groups in general and the gay minority in particular. And homosexual students—and there are such students in every classroom—may be denied accurate, gay-affirmative information and materials, as well as the support and guidance of a much-needed role model. It is no wonder, then, that closeted teachers so often feel torn. Yet the fear of harassment from students and parents, the fear of discrimination by other teachers and administrators, and the fear of dismissal by the school system itself remain in the forefront of their minds. It remains unclear, though, just how likely it is that such a negative outcome will actually result when a gay teacher does come forward with his sexual orientation.

Historically, of course, a negative outcome would have been very likely. Researcher Karen Harbeck, PhD, JD, explains that teachers in colonial times were expected to be the bearers of traditional knowledge and conventional morality and for this reason were sometimes forbidden to date, marry, have children, drink alcohol, smoke cigarettes, or dance; proscriptions similar to those of the clergy.[4] Obviously, teachers today are granted far more latitude, yet there remains within the general population the expectation that they serve as exemplars of morality, this from a populace that still largely considers the same-sex orientation to be a sign of moral bankruptcy. Thus, teachers who remain in the closet may have fears that are, in some instances, at least partly grounded in reality. And often, they anticipate the harshest judgments from the students themselves.

Recently, I asked an acquaintance who teaches eighth grade at an inner-city school in New Orleans if he had come out to the students in his classes. "Are you kidding?" he answered. "They'd savage me, they'd savage me!" He added, however, that virtually all of the teachers at his school, as well as the principal, have long known that he is gay and seem to have no problem with it. Furthermore, this same acquaintance is very much *out* in the gay community and routinely involved in gay political issues at the municipal level.

Coming Out in American Schools

In terms of formal research on the subject, Pat Griffin at the University of Massachusetts studied fifteen gay and lesbian educators to determine the ways in which they managed their sexual identities at work, as well as the effects of their participation in a gay empowerment group.[5] In addition to the two researchers, the group under study included ten teachers, a principal, a guidance counselor, and a librarian. All but one were Caucasian, with an age range of thirty-six to forty-five years. And while none of the teachers were entirely closeted, none were publicly out at their schools, either.

In the group discussions, it became apparent that the educators shared several worries about coming out on the job. In addition to the concerns mentioned above—the fear of harassment, discrimination, and job termination—they were worried that physical contact with their students might be misconstrued as having sexual overtones and lead to accusations of attempted child molestation. They were also concerned that, were they to be helpful to gay students, they might be charged with attempting to recruit these youths. And they feared that if they were to come out in the classroom, they might lose credibility with their students, and along with it, respect and authority.

As for the ways in which these educators managed their gay identities on the job, for the most part they dealt with the matter on a situational basis: they made decisions about how to handle the fact of their sexual orientation with particular people and in specific circumstances as they arose. They did not appear to develop overall identity management plans—especially not proactive or "coming-out" strategies—conceived in advance, put into action, then assessed for effectiveness. Instead, their preparation focused on what to do when confronted or accused of being homosexual; a plan for self-defense. The participants also said that they felt a sense of "self-betrayal" by keeping their sexual dispositions so close to the vest and wished that they were more able to incorporate their same-sex orientations into their professional identities.

In terms of specific management styles, this group of educators described four ways in which they handle their sexual identities at work, with most of them using a combination of methods, depending on the circumstances. As could be expected, some said that they attempt to "pass," meaning that they intentionally mislead others into assuming that they are straight, while others said that they try to "cover" their orientations—that while they do not deliberately misrepresent themselves as heterosexual, neither do they furnish any information that might lead others to conclude that they're gay. Still others said that they are "implicitly" out of the closet, a strategy in which they talk frankly about their lives and relationships and let other people draw their own conclusions but without actually saying at any point, "I'm gay." In some respects, this is akin to "dropping hints," a subtle way of informing others that one is homosexual without risking a full-fledged, irreversible acknowledgment. And finally, a few described themselves as being "explicitly" out. Yet to this group, being explicitly out did not mean going public with their sexual dispositions, but rather revealing their orientations to certain trustworthy colleagues. As far as actually coming out to a student, only two educators had done so, although some had confided in former pupils. Apparently none of the educators had ever come out to a classroom full of students.

Regarding the conditions in which these individuals were most likely to divulge their same-sex orientations, as could be expected, they said that they were more inclined to do it in settings where they felt relatively safe and in charge, such as in private or in their offices. They were also more apt to come out to colleagues whom they trusted, potential allies who were perhaps known for being particularly accepting of minorities. And they were more likely to open up to students who were struggling with issues related to their own sexual identities.

Coming Out in Dutch Schools

Of course, gay teachers exist outside of the United States as well, and research from other nations is informative. Peter Dankmeijer at the University of Amsterdam, for instance, interviewed ten gay male teachers about the ways in which they dealt with their same-sex orientations while on the job and found that they managed their sexual identities in one of three ways.[6]

In the first strategy, which Dr. Dankmeijer labels "normal," the teachers developed classroom styles that conformed to conventional societal expectations, the result being that their sexual orientations were essentially invisible. These educators "did not feel themselves very homosexual" and felt that "homosexuality was only a label put upon them by others,"[7] a rather unusual perspective. On the job, these individuals did not feel discriminated against, nor did they become as indignant about episodes of discrimination as did their colleagues, including their heterosexual colleagues.

The second method of identity management, "camp," Dr. Dankmeijer applies to those male teachers who intentionally came across in a humorous, apparently somewhat feminine, manner in the classroom as a way of challenging traditional sex-role stereotypes. While they did not actually come out as gay men, these individuals did consider their amusing behavior to be an implicit call for the tolerance of individual differences and employed a congenial personal style to win over those who otherwise might be opposed to such unconventional behavior. As could be expected, these instructors were at times discriminated against because their manner of presenting themselves clashed with established gender-specific codes of conduct.

And lastly, Dr. Dankmeijer assigns the term "gay" to those educators who were politically aware and publicly forthright about their same-sex dispositions, a group that included gay activists. This was the only group of teachers that considered the act of coming out to be a meaningful and affirmative political gesture. Unfortunately, these individuals were also likely to be subjected to antigay discrimination because of their frank discussions of human sexuality and their outspoken support of progressive social and political ideologies.

In terms of equitable treatment on the job, then, studies such as this one suggest that it is safer for a homosexual instructor to downplay, if not largely deny the existence of, his same-sex orientation while on the job. We could assume, though, that those teachers who are truly out of the closet, those who knowingly risk negative judgments in order to air their opinions and express their sexual dispositions candidly, are motivated by concerns beyond those of simple job security. Which brings us to the matter of on-the-job discrimination and the rights of the openly gay teacher.

Gay Teachers and the Law

As we have noted, Western society, in times past, permitted teachers little behavioral leeway and even today expects them to be emissaries of traditional morality. Nevertheless, we live in an age marked by an emerging respect for both human diversity and workplace rights, such that the chances of a teacher being blatantly discriminated against or terminated outright for being gay appear to be fading at last. To determine the extent to which this is true, Dr. Harbeck, in a fine review, traced the history of legal sanctions against homosexual educators in the United States during the twentieth century and discovered an increasing tolerance of gay teachers, or at least a growing unwillingness on the part of school districts to attempt to fire them or revoke their credentials.[8] Also noted was an unwillingness by the judiciary to support such harsh actions.

Indeed, while earlier this century homosexual instructors were simply forced out of their jobs, beginning in the 1950s and more frequently in the 1960s and 1970s, the judiciary came to view citizens' personal lives, including those of teachers, to be private matters beyond the authority of the government. As for sexual conduct in particular, during this period the judiciary began to regard sex acts between consenting adults to be, for the most part, an inappropriate arena for its involvement. Accordingly, the objections to gay teachers that might have been registered by school districts in the past no longer enjoyed the backing of the criminal justice system.

In terms of specific actions, Dr. Harbeck noted a 1969 landmark California case, *Morrison vs. State Board of Education*, which concluded that "the status of being a homosexual was insufficient grounds for dismissal unless coupled with some related misbehavior."[9] Also significant was the 1979 decision by the National Education Association to add sexual orientation to its list of characteristics to be protected from discrimination. Both actions helped shield gay teachers from unfair treatment.

More recently, the matter of teachers' sexual orientations has come to be interpreted by many educators as a civil rights issue, with constitutional guarantees of equal treatment under the law being at stake. But the courts have not yet provided a definitive ruling in this matter. Dr. Harbeck says the following:

> Because of the complexities of the legal and social issues, and because of the seemingly limitless legal and financial resources on both sides, the courts appear to have tried to avoid a direct declaration concerning whether or not gay men and lesbians have a constitutional right to teach school. . . . School boards seem more than willing to look the other way with respect to a teacher's sexual orientation unless some indiscretion has occurred, and they certainly seem to be more willing to negotiate than to face the costly expense of litigation.[10]

She adds that attempts to revoke gay teachers' credentials have virtually disappeared in recent times.

Thus, it would appear that there may be several ways in which a teacher who comes out on the job may defend himself if he faces discrimination. But from the available literature, it seems that gay educators may be not be all that aware of their relative safety at work, particularly those who work with older children and who are tenured. In fact, teachers typically seem to expect the worst if they come forward, when instead they might have a more favorable experience. While there is presently a relative lack of data on this matter, the group empowerment study that we discussed earlier does address this point to a certain degree.[11]

That group, which met regularly over a period of fifteen months, resulted in several positive changes in its members. Among other gains, the participants became more aware of the ways in which they previously had been oppressed both by their school systems and their own fears, with some of them becoming deeply angered by this insight. As a result, they began to feel more entitled. As well, the educators reported feeling more integrated as a result of the group experience, with their sexual identities now being better incorporated into their professional identities. And they felt less fearful about being homosexual on the job. "Without exception all participants believed that they were speaking out more in school about homophobia and being more open about their lesbian and gay identities," noted the author of that report.[12] "Every action taken was carefully evaluated to assess the consequences, and most often participants were amazed at the lack of negative responses they received from colleagues and students." Two of the group members subsequently came out to their colleagues, while another came out to both colleagues and students.

To continue this productive process and extend it to other gay educators, at the conclusion of the group project the participants formed an organization, an important aim of which was to arrange monthly discussion groups for professionals throughout the area. Early reports suggest that the groups were well-attended and productive. It would seem, then, that imparting useful information and providing peer support may help gay educators, as minority members, become more mindful of their employment circumstances, assist them in better incorporating their sexual orientations into their professional identities, and help them come further out of the closet while on the job. In this manner, such openly homosexual educators are actually assisting all of their gay colleagues in the teaching profession acquire both the respect and the guarantee of rights that they deserve and, indeed, should fully expect in a democratic society.

THE SCIENCES

Regarding other occupations, most gay men, whether in or out of the closet, hold positions that require contact mainly with other adults. For this reason, society's groundless concerns that have so often haunted gay men in child-related professions do not apply to those who work in these fields. This does not mean, however, that these gentlemen are free from antigay bias; on the contrary, prejudice just wears different masks in these fields.

One might assume, for instance, that in the scientific community a person's sexual orientation would be immaterial, and this may or may not be the case for the researcher who spends much of his time in the laboratory. But for the gay man who is engaged in other forms of scientific inquiry, such as the social scientist whose work takes him into the world at large, the issue of his sexual disposition may continue to assert itself.

The Role of the Scientist

As it stands, the basis for this concern about expressing one's sexual identity on the job has to do with the way in which the role of the scientist has been defined historically. The traditional view of the scientist is that of an academic who purposely establishes a distance between himself and that which he is investigating in order to examine the subject matter objectively and attain a valid insight into it. Accordingly, disciplines ranging from astronomy to microbiology have long insisted that a researcher detach himself from the phenomenon under analysis, this being a key component of the scientific method, a convention of Western empiricism.

As for the social sciences—those fields of study concerned with relationships within a society—this insistence upon distancing oneself from the focus of inquiry has meant that investigators are expected to reveal little, if anything, about themselves to those whom they are researching or perhaps assisting, so as to avoid inviting personal reactions and thus contaminating their work. For the social scientist who happens to be gay, this has been taken to mean that he should guard his sexual orientation while on the job, since in societies in which homosexuality continues to be a controversial matter—Judeo-Christian societies like our own, for instance—it is assumed that such information could markedly affect people's reactions to him and alter the course of his work. For many gay social scientists today, then, being in the closet may not be so much a matter of personal choice as a dictate of protocol.

That said, a growing number of scientists now consider this unquestioned faith in the traditional scientific method to be questionable in itself. They see this allegiance to presumed objectivity as a way in which scientists delude themselves into believing that they are truly independent agents, when, in fact, they are not. Accordingly, many fields of inquiry are revisiting the issue. In physics, for instance, theorists have been rethinking their positions for several years now, since discoveries in quantum physics revealed that an observer is never entirely separate from that which he chooses to observe; that the investigator, whether or not he is aware of it, is an important part of the phenomenon under investigation, a dynamic player. Only by realizing this fact and taking it into account when designing his research and analyzing its findings can he begin to truly understand the subject matter. In this line of thinking, then, we are viewed as human beings first, scientists second, and as such are intricately related to every other aspect of our world, an interactive state of affairs that we must take into account if we are to make genuine progress in our scientific endeavors.

Applying this notion to the social sciences, it suggests that gay professionals, such as sociologists and psychologists, who are required to interact with other people as a routine part of their work could, at times, gain much by acknowledging openly their personal characteristics as researchers or practitioners. This might entail coming out to those under study or treatment, an act that would have been unthinkable in either profession only a short time ago.

The Field of Anthropology

As an example, in the field of anthropology—specifically, that branch of anthropology concerned with cultural origins, growth, and change, called *ethnology*—gay fieldworkers have often concealed their sexual orientations from the members of the societies they have studied, for seemingly valid reasons. Even more rigorously, they have kept their same-sex dispositions out of their professional writings. Of course, their straight colleagues have likewise shied away from mentioning their heterosexuality in their written accounts despite living, sometimes for years, with those of other cultures in remote corners of the world and at times becoming affectionately and even sexually engaged with those they studied. Such involvements may occur, for instance, when an ethnographer takes part in a traditional social custom that consists of a symbolic act that is erotic in nature, or when, after a long period of relative isolation in the field, he develops a longing for a person in his immediate surroundings. In such an event, it could be argued that the researcher has adopted a participant-observer position, but without acknowledging or conveying this fact to his readers. Consequently, a problem exists in the writings of a certain portion of ethnographers, an incompleteness in their reports, in that their sexual orientations, interests, and actions in the field are missing from their otherwise comprehensive accounts of the societies they observe. And while this censoring of the sexual may simply reflect a dated provincialism in the field, it is also related to the expectation that the anthropologist portray himself as an individual having academic interests only, a perpetuation of the illusion of the social scientist as a detached, objective observer. Yet today, a growing number of gay ethnographers are taking issue with this convention.

"Anthropologists have incorporated the worst aspects of Victorian prudery in avoiding an honest assessment of their sexual behaviors in the field," writes ethnographer Walter Williams.[13] This anthropologist, himself gay with a background in Native American studies, took a sabbatical to study American Indians who are homosexual. Early on, he came out to one of his principal contacts, a tribal historian, who, now trusting the researcher, helped him launch the study. "After I identified myself as gay, that man agreed to talk with me about his life. He said he would not have opened up if I had been the typical heterosexual anthropologist,"[14] says Williams. "In that experience, as with numerous others since then, I feel that I have had an enormous advantage in doing my fieldwork by being openly gay." In this case, the research resulted in an intriguing book, titled *The Spirit and the Flesh,* a study of the *two-spirited* people—homosexual individuals—in Native American society.

As could be expected, the gay anthropologist who remains closeted, sidestepping personal questions and perhaps appearing asexual, may cause members of the host society to be suspicious of him, the result being that they withhold from him crucial information about their beliefs and customs. By comparison, presenting himself forthrightly as a gay man may facilitate trust and the formation of productive relationships and thus foster the sharing of important cultural information. It should be noted, too, that coming out in other societies is not necessarily a risky act. In many of them, especially those that have escaped the influence of Western missionaries, same-sex affection is a vital feature of the community, such that being openly gay in such settings is entirely acceptable. It is such facts, say an increasing number of gay anthropologists, that should be reported in ethnographers' accounts of their work, since this sort of information is indispensable in genuinely understanding a host society and the researcher's interactions with it. Furthermore, material of this type can be of inestimable value in preparing future ethnographers for the further exploration of such societies.

Of course, anthropologists, while being painstakingly accurate in their written accounts, must also be careful to protect, when necessary, the sexual identities of those whom they describe in their work. Certainly in some societies, particularly Western ones, publicly exposing an individual's same-sex nature can be very damaging. Care should therefore be taken in this regard. Likewise, care should be taken when introducing the subject of one's own homosexual orientation into one's professional writing, so that the reasons for its presence in such reports is understood by readers. In some instances, this may involve acknowledging the growing opinion among contemporary gay researchers that by identifying one's own sexual disposition and perhaps discussing its role in the selection and interpretation of material from the field, as well as by balancing one's "objective" observations with this relevant personal information, the quality of one's reports may be enhanced immeasurably.

In the final analysis, this dialogue in anthropology as to the need for greater honesty and frankness in acknowledging sexual matters, as well as the positive effects such forthrightness may have on accuracy and completeness in reporting, illustrates one of the ways in which openly gay researchers, by pursuing the issues raised by their sexual orientations, may contribute to progress in the scientific arena and, ultimately, to the advancement of society itself.

BUSINESS AND INDUSTRY

Gay men may also advance society through their contributions in the business world, both in terms of the quality and quantity of their work and through their visibility as gay professionals. By being candid and accessible, they can help educate heterosexual co-workers, while serving as role models for their more closeted peers.

In terms of career choices, a 1991 national survey found that the majority of gay people in the United States hold managerial, health care, and educational positions.[15] As for their degree of openness on the job, most of those in the business community disclose their same-sex orientations to at least one other person in the workplace, with a smaller number coming out at a broad organizational level. The preponderance of gay workers say that they prefer to remain partially closeted, and they cite two principal reasons for this decision.

First, a gay person may be closeted in all areas of his life and, for this reason, worry that if he makes known his same-sex disposition on the job, people outside the workplace may hear about it, including perhaps his family members and acquaintances. He may therefore need to deal with the matter in his personal life before doing so at work. The fact is, most men come out on the job only after they have discussed their same-sex orientations with their families and friends and feel comfortable being gay in private life. They may even depend on their loved ones' behind-the-scenes encouragement and support to bolster them when coming forward in the work setting.

Second, most closeted men in the business world are concerned about the career damage that being openly gay might bring, a realistic consideration in many cases. We must remember that, in extreme circumstances, a person's livelihood may be at stake if he reveals his same-sex orientation at work—and not only his present income, but possibly his future employability as well. For this reason, a substantial number of men are simply unwilling, as they see it, to put their careers on the line by disclosing this information about themselves in the work setting.

Other businessmen, while not worried about being fired, are concerned with hitting the "lavender ceiling," that organizational level above which a homosexual man may not be permitted to advance. It is thought, for instance, that in certain conservative businesses gay men are not placed in positions in which they might be called upon to serve as company spokesmen or otherwise represent their firms in the public arena because those at the executive level do not want these gentlemen's sexual orientations to become associated with the companies' images. Yet even when the executive tier is comfortable with personal diversity and organizational heterogeneity, there may still be an overarching concern that its clientele might feel ill at ease doing business with openly gay representatives of the company. Accordingly, the homosexual employee may not be promoted to such a highly visible and influential position even though he may be the most qualified person for the job.

A related concern is harassment. Especially in socially and politically backward organizations, a gay staff member may become the butt of jokes or the victim of slander. If he is seen talking to another gay male employee, much less becoming friends with that person, their platonic alliance may quickly become fodder for gossip and scandal. In fact, in a highly conservative, autocratic organization, a pretext may even be concocted for separating the two employees for fear that they may become intimately involved, this issuing from the outdated notion that homosexual men are "oversexed" and cannot be trusted to be together for a significant length of time. Of course, such beliefs are not only seriously mistaken, but also insulting to the individuals involved, both professionally and personally, and the resultant action against them, repugnant. Yet the fact remains that there are still many ill-informed individuals who subscribe to such hackneyed beliefs and who feel morally entitled to act on their flawed assumptions.

Over the years, I have known of troubling instances in which gay men have been followed on the job—literally—by their ostensibly straight supervisors simply because the supervisors were preoccupied with the notion that these men might be "up to something," despite clear evidence refuting such a likelihood. I have also known of gay men who have found their desks or offices rifled through after business hours with no similar searches being conducted on their straight colleagues—again, with no known justification. And while such unwarranted intrusions are apparently infrequent in most healthy organizations, when they do occur, they nearly always cause the gay worker to become distraught and to spend much time worrying about his circumstances, time that he would otherwise devote to fulfilling his job responsibilities. Consequently, the worker in such straits may find his morale, loyalty, and job performance suffering over time, which may, in turn, limit his professional prospects in the future. By comparison, the heterosexual employee does not have to contend with this brand of destructive, prejudicial treatment, nor must he cope with the stress brought about by such implicit threats to his livelihood or the career damage that may ultimately result from his convoluted employment situation.

These instances in which gay workers are wronged on the job are most often the result of ignorance and bigotry. In some cases, however, they may also stem from the sexual conflicts of heterosexual workers, or deeply closeted homosexual workers, being projected onto them. Regardless of the cause, though, the point is that such abuse does occur at certain times and in certain settings and that many gay workers, rather than challenging it, remain in hiding and endure the mistreatment. Often, they are unwilling to act for fear of retaliation. Some men, particularly those who insist on preserving their personal integrity and who feel strongly about their rights as individuals, *do* come forward, however, and confront such offenses. In fact, in surveys conducted in the business community, gay men as a group offer a profusion of reasons for coming out on the job, ranging from the desire to contest discrimination and persecution to the need for personal and professional growth in the workplace.

Reasons for Coming Out

Understandably, some gay men, over the course of time, tire of concealing their affectional and sexual orientations for forty-plus hours a week. Satisfied with being gay and perhaps assuming that their co-workers have long since caught on anyway, they find no compelling reason to continue the pretense. Accordingly, they decide to come forward and deal with whatever resistance they may encounter. Many other gay men, however, offer more narrowly defined reasons for disclosing their sexual orientations in the business world.

Relationship Development

A man may feel the need to divulge this information about himself in order to define the parameters of a particular relationship in the workplace. In other cases, he may feel the need to share this aspect of himself as part of the normal and predictable desire to relate meaningfully, and reciprocally, to others.

As for the former—establishing relationship boundaries—the man may feel, for example, that it is best that his female co-workers understand that he is homosexual so that they will not think of him as a potential romantic partner or, conversely, so that they will feel sexually secure with him when they are away on business trips together or in similar circumstances. He may decide, too, that his male co-workers should know about his sexual disposition, so that, among other things, they will not try to "fix him up" with an available female worker; as well, so they will take into account his orientation when planning functions such as all-male events that might involve entertaining women after hours, a bonding ritual in certain types of organizations.

As for the need for honesty and social reciprocity, the gay employee, typically spending dozens of hours each week with his co-workers, may become emotionally close to them and wish to relate to them more fully. This is a natural and predictable course of events. Similarly, his colleagues themselves may, over time, share more and more information about themselves with him and may rightfully expect the man to do likewise. Indeed, for him not to reciprocate could well impede the growth and development of these relationships. At some point, then, the gay worker usually feels the need to open up to his colleagues about his sexual orientation as a reflection of his regard for them. It also reflects his recognition of, and attempts to comply with, established social conventions.

Another reason that a man may divulge this information to someone in the organization—specifically, to another man—is because he wishes to explore the possibility of developing an intimate relationship with him. Regardless of sexual orientation, countless individuals meet and fall in love on the job, with an enormous number of marriages and other forms of long-term commitment resulting from these initial encounters. This should come as no surprise, given that most adults in our society spend the bulk of their daytime hours in work settings with other adults. And while some companies try to discourage the development of such relationships, arguing that they interfere with job performance, other companies take the opposite position, believing that emotionally gratified, "attached" adults make the best employees. Progressive organizations may even sponsor company mixers or other types of gatherings for their single workers to help them meet and establish personal relationships. Of course, gay mixers are unheard of at most companies; no formal attempts are made to introduce homosexual employees to one another. Nevertheless, like a heterosexual man and woman on the job, gay men do occasionally meet in work settings and go on to develop intimate relationships outside of the office. And in such cases, the men, at some point, must make known to one another their sexual orientations; this ordinarily occurs in the workplace itself.

Life Circumstances

At other times, events in the man's life may compel him to reveal his sexual disposition. His long-term relationship with his partner may come to an end, for example, and like a heterosexual employee struggling through a separation or divorce, he may experience all manner of painful and disruptive emotions. For this reason, he may feel the need to explain his emotional state to those with whom he works, requiring that he come out to them. In other cases, the man or his partner may develop an ailment of some sort, such as HIV-related illness, resulting in occasional absences from work; accordingly, the employee divulges his sexual orientation as a way of explaining how this medical event is affecting his life. Finally, a gay worker may wish to include his same-sex partner on his insurance policy or seek other types of domestic partner benefits and, for this reason, reveals his sexual orientation.

Job-Related Benefits

In still other instances, gay men are aware of the career advantages that being *out* on the job may present—and, indeed, there may be several benefits. By coming forward as homosexual, a man may be viewed as confident, honest, and trustworthy. Moreover, he cannot be exposed as gay, so there is no chance of his being blackmailed by competitors. In such a case, then, coming out may evince character and principle, while at the same time preventing a potentially damaging exposé from taking place.

By comparison, the worker who remains closeted, if his sexual orientation is eventually discovered, may be held in low regard by his peers, not necessarily because he is gay, but because of his decision to mislead them about it. Consequently, in the future he may not be trusted. Furthermore, while in the closet, the man may have to live with the unnerving prospect of being exposed at any time, a worry that may render him unwilling to stand up to certain persons or policies in the organization for fear of unseemly retribution.

Additional job-related benefits include the fact that the openly gay worker may be considered a unique asset to the company due to his knowledge of the homosexual community. Increasingly, firms are seeking entry into the gay and lesbian market since homosexual men and women, as a group, have a higher than average disposable income. The astute gay employee, then, can be of enormous value since he is in a position to help his organization understand and approach this potential source of business. In some cases, he may even serve as a direct liaison to the gay community itself, something that might be much more difficult for a heterosexual worker.

The openly gay employee is also in a position to network with other gay workers and their organizations, thus enhancing his company's, and his own, reach in numerous ways. But again, to be an active member of such networks, the man must be forthright about his sexual orientation.

Political Circumstances

Of course, political considerations may also compel one to come forward. This most often occurs when an employee finds himself or other homosexual workers the victims of discrimination. On an individual basis, it may occur when the man develops symptoms of HIV disease, for instance, and the organization fails to respond responsibly to his circumstances. On a collective basis, it may happen when gay employees, as a group, are limited by company policies that treat them unjustly, whether by oversight or design. In such cases, the gay worker intentionally reveals his same-sex orientation, then goes on record with his political position because he considers the long-term gains to be worth it.

In addition, there are those men who come out on the job because they feel a responsibility to serve as role models for closeted gays, and not necessarily for those who are younger. Today, many youthful homosexual employees are, in fact, functioning as role models for an older generation of gay men, men who came of age at a time when a businessman was required to dissociate entirely his homosexual orientation from his professional identity and who may now need to learn how to be more open at work.

Lastly, a man may come out so that he can educate his heterosexual colleagues. This may occur either as a spontaneous, perhaps even a defensive, reaction to their antigay remarks or as a gradual, informative process planned in advance and implemented in a stepwise manner. Regardless of the way in which it is done, though, the aim is the same: to improve the organizational environment by making it a more accepting, productive, and equitable setting for the gay worker.

Levels of Coming Out

As for the precise ways in which homosexual businessmen come out on the job, many disclose their orientations to only one or a few co-workers, while others reveal themselves at a more general level. In this regard, a study by Annette Friskopp and Sharon Silverstein is edifying.[16] These women interviewed over a hundred gay and lesbian Harvard MBAs between 1991 and 1994 and, based on the information they collected, described the strategies and effects of coming out both narrowly and broadly.

Interestingly, they found that the majority of their interviewees did not plan in advance how they would come out on the job, a rather unexpected finding given that this group of professionals was otherwise well-organized and forward-looking. When it came to their own sexual orientations, however, they were not inclined to look ahead and formulate strategies for divulging their sexual dispositions in the workplace, this despite the fact that many of them spoke of their meticulous preparations for coming out to their families and friends in private life.

Coming Out Narrowly

As it turns out, those who were least likely to plan a coming-out strategy were the most likely to disclose their same-sex orientations to only a few co-workers. And in those instances in which these individuals *did* contemplate beforehand how they would reveal this information about themselves, the issue was often framed in terms of how they would try to manage the situation if their sexual orientations were to be discovered by others.

Of course, some MBAs came out selectively for other reasons. For instance, there were those who believed that it was inappropriate to divulge their sexual and affectional dispositions to their subordinates, since this might blur the distinction between their roles and alter the balance of power. And indeed, in some settings it is considered improper and potentially troublesome to reveal significant personal information about oneself, sexual or otherwise, to subordinates because of the long-standing belief that it will diminish one's authority and influence. Still, this relatively common organizational practice is not necessarily a valid one. It could be argued that professional respect is gained not by hiding information from other people, but by the manner in which one presents it. The point, however, is that some closeted businessmen use this traditional emphasis on privacy as a reason, or an excuse, to conceal their same-sex dispositions from those in their work environments.

Regarding the act of coming out itself, Friskopp and Silverstein noted that when gay workers who use a narrow approach encounter negative reactions from other people, they sometimes give up their efforts. By failing to anticipate the possibility of such unfavorable responses, they find themselves unable to proceed, at least temporarily.

Coming Out Broadly

In contrast to those who lacked a well-developed coming-out plan, those gay workers who did devise proactive strategies were more likely to come out broadly, often at an organizational level. In some instances, they entered their companies as openly gay, informing others of this fact during the initial interviews and continuing to do so during their early days or weeks on the job. Others came forward at an extensive level after a longer association with the company. As for the strategies themselves, they were typically designed around declaring homosexuality in a vital, positive manner as opposed to "self-defense" plans that focused only on the possibility of a discovery or other type of involuntary exposure.

As for unfavorable reactions, this study found that when gay people having well-planned, systematic strategies for coming out on the job encountered negative reactions, they tended to continue coming forward anyway. This is because they anticipated the occasional contrary response and did not let it prevent them from achieving their objective. Instead, they typically reassessed their strategies and modified them for better results.

Finally, Friskopp and Silverstein looked at the characteristics and circumstances of those who were most likely to come out on the job and found that such individuals were generally comfortable being gay, had already revealed their sexual orientations to their families and friends, and in many cases had life partners. As well, they tended to receive encouragement and support from other gay people for their coming-out efforts in the workplace and had well-organized plans for doing so. They also felt that their work settings were neutral or perhaps even friendly toward gay people.

Styles of Coming Out

Other researchers have looked at the actual methods men use when they come out in the professional arena. James Woods and Jay Lucas, for instance, conducted seventy interviews during 1990 and 1991 with a well-educated group of middle- to upper-middle-class gay men, most of whom were Caucasian, lived in or near large urban centers, and were generally liberal in their views.[17] While an array of professionals was included in the study, a substantial share consisted of those in the field of business. In their interviews, Woods and Lucas observed various styles of coming out, ranging from those methods that were rather timid and tenuous to those that were bold and confident.

The first coming-out strategy the researchers refer to as *minimizing visibility* and is an indirect approach. It may be accomplished, for instance, by mentioning one's same-sex partner or otherwise dropping hints on the job, the gay man being unwilling to discuss openly his same-sex orientation because he is fearful that he may offend or alienate his heterosexual co-workers. In some cases, we could assume that such a worker may be apprehensive without cause; that he might be surprised to find that his colleagues are much more comfortable with his sexual orientation than he imagines, if it even matters to them at all. Nevertheless, being fearful, he approaches the matter gingerly.

The second method, *normalizing the abnormal,* Woods and Lucas describe as an effort at assimilation in which the gay employee strives to make his sexual orientation appear as an ordinary, unremarkable aspect of his life to those with whom he works. His goal is to present himself as very much akin to his heterosexual co-workers with the exception of his sexual disposition, yet with even this feature of himself not being all that different. To this end, the gay man may try to correct popular misconceptions about homosexual men and their lives, replacing mistaken ideas with accurate facts. That is, he may attempt to deconstruct the myth of the "gay lifestyle," supplanting it with images of gay men's actual ways of life, which, in most respects, are the same as those of straight people. Through such an approach, he hopes that he will better fit into the workplace. Woods and Lucas explain that, in this strategy, the person's aim is "to normalize his identity, to make homosexuality the functional equivalent of heterosexuality," so that he may attain equality on the job.[18]

Dignifying difference is a third style of coming out in the work setting, one in which the man embraces the fact that, in certain respects, he *is* different from his heterosexual peers and seeks to highlight the advantages of this distinction. In essence, he turns his minority status into a condition that yields tangible benefits. The person using such a strategy does not feel a strong need to assimilate into the heterosexually dominated work environment, at least not in the sense of forfeiting his identity as a gay person. Rather, he wishes to preserve this personal characteristic and put it to work for him.

Earlier we mentioned the benefits of being an openly homosexual businessman when one's company wishes to tap into the gay consumer market. In such a case, the gay worker may use to his advantage his knowledge, experience, and contacts in the homosexual community in order to advance his company's interests. A person visibly putting to use his same-sex orientation in this manner, then, may be *dignifying difference.*

In other cases, the individual's unique social and emotional development as a gay person may have a positive impact on his abilities in the workplace. Growing up gay, learning to cope with widespread antagonism because of it, and overcoming the myriad of obstacles brought about by one's unpopular sexual orientation usually requires that a person develop an array of special qualities over the years, attributes that he may then adapt to his work. By trading on this fact, then, he may be using a dignifying strategy.

Lastly, Woods and Lucas describe a fourth approach, *politicizing marginality*—a confrontational style that becomes necessary in certain settings or under specific conditions. In a hostile workplace, for instance, the gay worker may need to challenge certain aspects of the system, from first-hand prejudicial treatment by his superiors to formal policies and procedures that discriminate against homosexual employees. Thus, the gay man uses his marginality to acquire political gains, either for himself or for other gay employees.

Of course, many organizations are not particularly fond of employees who are politically active in the workplace, especially those who are homosexual. The fact is, many companies prefer that their gay workers keep low profiles or, better yet, not come out of the closet at all. Accordingly, the *out* and politically involved gay worker may be perceived as a threat to the company, an instrument of unwanted change. Be that as it may, the man himself typically considers his assertive approach to be essential and, in the long term, helpful. He comes forward on the job as an act of social and political conscience, and he does so conspicuously.

Other Considerations

Ultimately, the gay businessman must take into account several factors when contemplating coming out on the job. Foremost is the climate of the work setting itself. In a highly conservative environment in which employees seldom divulge any sort of personal information about themselves, a sweeping declaration of one's homosexuality may be met with bewilderment, hostility, and even attempts at censure. By comparison, in a more liberal setting in which workers freely discuss themselves and their loved ones, and in which openly gay employees thrive, coming out may be met with easy acceptance and genuine support. Generally, it appears that the degree of acceptance in most business settings falls somewhere between these two poles, with the preponderance of organizations being neither entirely rejecting nor accepting. The gay worker must therefore gauge the political mood of his particular company, the degree of openness shown by other gay employees, and any unique advantages or disadvantages that coming out in this setting may involve before deciding if, and how, to proceed. This applies to gay workers in nonbusiness career fields as well. For that matter, much of what we have discussed in this section is germane to those in other vocational areas.

As a rule, of course, it is preferable to come out in the workplace whenever feasible and to as many people as realistically possible. Studies of those men who have done so, while acknowledging the resistance they sometimes encounter in the process, have shown that most of them are truly glad, in the long run, that they came forward. Indeed, research indicates that gay men tend to experience less depression and anxiety after coming out on the job, as well as enhanced self-esteem,[19] findings that are consistent with those discussed in Chapter 2 in which gay men who were married to women and later divorced reported declines in medical problems and improvements in mental health. Coming out on the job, then, while involving varying levels of risk, for most men eventually results in a greater sense of well-being and self-respect. That said, it is important to bear in mind that, in some fields, homosexual men do not have the option to come forward and receive such benefits, most notably those who are members of organizations like the United States military, an institution known for its inflexibility and past discrimination against minority groups.

THE MILITARY

At any given time, a substantial number of citizens wishes to enter the armed forces, some because of deeply rooted patriotic leanings and others for strictly practical reasons. The fact is, since our nation has not recently involved itself in a major foreign war, many men now pursue military service in order to receive specialized training while collecting wages and benefits. They see a stint in the service as a combination training program and temporary job and as something that will serve them well after they leave the service. Of course, for thousands of others the military is much more than a temporary occupation: it is a lifelong career. The armed forces, then, attract a sizable share of the population and provides it with both short-term and long-term job opportunities, one of several functions it has served throughout this century.

Unfortunately, throughout this century the military has also found itself embroiled in social and legal conflicts, including drawn-out controversies stemming from allegations of injustice and discrimination against minority groups, despite the fact that the armed forces are in place to protect a nation in which all citizens are purportedly equal. And such charges of unfairness persist even today, as evidenced by the ongoing dispute about gays in the military.

As it stands, for the citizen who enlists and who happens to be homosexual—and up to 10 percent of all service personnel are, in fact, gay, according to a Pentagon report[20]—the military experience can be a distressing one. According to the policy established by President Clinton in 1993, a gay serviceman cannot come forward at any point while he is in the military and state that he is homosexual without being discharged or, in more extreme cases, court-martialed, nor may he have sex with another man at any time during his service commitment, regardless of whether the experience takes place on-base or off-base. Of course, such profound injunctions against free speech and intimate behavior do not apply to heterosexual personnel; certainly the straight population would never stand for such gross infringements of its rights. But when it comes to gay servicemen, they are not considered to have such rights.

As it is currently constructed, then, the policy of the United States military is, by most accounts, critically flawed. And it appears that the judiciary may agree: courts have begun ruling against it, including a federal court that has concluded that the policy is unconstitutional, a decision the White House plans to appeal.

Research on the Performance of Gay Military Personnel

For the record, it should be noted that there is no basis for believing that gay people cannot serve well in the military. They have done so for decades. As for formal research on the issue, all of the studies that have been commissioned by the Department of Defense have found gay men and women to perform in a satisfactory, if not an exemplary, fashion. These include the Crittendon Report, released in 1957, which concluded that gay men do not pose a security risk to the nation and are as qualified for service as straight men and the 1988 and 1989 Defense Personnel Security Research and Education Center (PERSEREC) studies, which found that, based on background information prior to entering the military, "the preponderance of the evidence . . . indicates that homosexuals show preservice suitability-related adjustment that is as good or better than the average heterosexual."[21] Even President Clinton, when announcing his decision to continue banning gays from military service, conceded that "there is no study showing (homosexual soldiers) to be less capable or more prone to misconduct than heterosexual soldiers. Indeed, all the information we have indicates that they are not less capable or more prone to misbehavior."[22]

Along these same lines, three recent studies by the General Accounting Office (1992, 1993) and the Rand Corporation (1993) found that gay citizens are altogether fit for military service, that sexual orientation, in and of itself, is irrelevant. Not surprisingly, this same conclusion has already been reached by several other nations as well, nations that today accept openly gay men into their militaries, among them Australia, Belgium, Canada, France, Germany, Israel, Japan, the Netherlands, Poland, Portugal, the Republic of Korea, South Africa, Spain, and Sweden. In this respect, the United States lags far behind nearly all other NATO nations.

The truth of the matter is that gay men are refused entry into the American military system because a certain portion of straight servicemen simply do not want them there, this being the basis for the claim voiced repeatedly by Bill Clinton and others that the presence of gay servicemen could "hurt morale." This is a feeble, time-worn argument, one that was previously used in an attempt to block the integration of Blacks and women into the armed forces and one that panders to the prejudices of heterosexual enlisted men rather than acknowledging and protecting the rights of a minority group that is, by all accounts, well qualified to serve.

Coming Out in the Military

As for disclosing one's sexual orientation in this setting, as we have noted, the current policy presents the gay man with an unacceptable choice: either forego all involvement in the military—participation and financial benefits to which he is arguably entitled by the Constitution—or mislead the military about his sexual orientation, hide in the closet, and remain vulnerable to blackmail or discharge. Which brings us to the question: Should a gay man enlist in the military, knowing its belligerently antigay climate and the current policy's ramifications? And if he does join, should he risk coming out to anyone once he is there?

In reality, a person who is fully aware that he is homosexual rarely, if ever, enlists with the intention of coming out officially once he is accepted. To do so is to guarantee discharge. Instead, the preponderance of gay men are either unaware that they are homosexual at the time of enlistment or they know that they are gay but plan to conceal this information throughout their military commitments.

In the former case, when a man discovers his same-sex orientation once he is already in the service, he typically remains in the military and fulfills his responsibilities while carefully guarding this information about himself. After a certain amount of time, however, he may find this an increasingly difficult posture to maintain and, for this reason, may consider telling someone about himself. In the latter case, the serviceman, knowing all along that he is gay but planning to keep this information hidden, after many months or years of emotional isolation may reconsider his decision to stay entirely closeted. In either case, the result is the same: the man feels a pressing need to come forward, a need to reveal his "secret" to another person. Yet doing so may cause problems, since the news of his orientation may travel well beyond its intended sphere and cause him irreparable damage.

The celebrated case of Joseph Steffan illustrates the point. Like many young men, Steffan was not fully aware that he was gay when he entered the United States Naval Academy in Annapolis, Maryland. Instead, he became aware of it only after he was already enrolled. Still, he did not act on his sexual feelings, but rather pursued his studies vigorously, distinguishing himself in the process. One of three top midshipmen in his class and a battalion commander in charge of six hundred others, a few months before graduation Steffan privately told two friends that he was homosexual. One of these friends, who was heterosexual, told his girlfriend, who then told her mother and father, who were acquainted with, and subsequently informed, an advisor to the superintendent of the Naval Academy. This sparked an investigation that culminated in Steffan being kicked out of the academy, along with threats of court-martial if he attempted to challenge the institution in court, which he did.[23] In this case, coming out to a friend in the context of a private conversation in a location off the military base led, through a circuitous route, to the disclosure being made known to authorities, and ultimately to harsh punishment. It is for such reasons that some gay servicemen are fearful of revealing their sexual orientations to anyone associated with the military.

And yet, many do come out to others but within certain limits. Indeed, only a very small percentage come forward formally, making the declaration to military officials and submitting to a discharge. Rather, most reveal themselves confidentially to specific individuals whom they know and trust. Yet, regardless of how the enlisted man does it, the decision itself is usually reached only after taking into account several important factors.

In this regard, the branch of the military to which the person belongs may be a consideration. It is widely believed, for instance, that different divisions of the armed forces demonstrate varying degrees of leniency on the matter, that the Army and Marine Corps, for instance, are among the most antagonistic toward homosexuality, while the Air Force is among the most tolerant. It is also thought to be riskier to come out to another serviceman when one is still in basic training and living in a barracks than when one has completed this training and is perhaps living in an apartment off-base. And it is believed that some locations, most notably certain foreign countries, offer environments that are broad-minded, permissive, and accepting of those of all orientations, while other environments are more oppressive, restrictive, and potentially hazardous to gay servicemen. Thus, when one contemplates disclosing his sexual orientation while in the armed forces, he may need to weigh these and other factors.

Coming Out Publicly

As for the man who decides to officially declare his homosexuality to the military authorities, as we have noted, his discharge is assured. But it is important to understand, as well, that the treatment he receives during this process may be unpredictable, as may be the amount of time that elapses before the discharge actually goes into effect.

The statements of a young man in the Air Force who officially acknowledged his sexual orientation and who was being dismissed for this reason are illuminating in this respect. In his case, coming out was a surprisingly lackluster event.

"(S)ince I made my, for lack of a better word, admission, nobody has been shocked or anything," he said.[24] "It was totally anticlimactic."

Yet, by way of comparison, this same serviceman recounted an Army case in which "they took this guy who had made his admission, out in front of his company, thirty or forty of his peers, made him stand up front, and announce to the company that he was gay, and that was why he has getting out. The charges were read at seven or eight different formations! It's a common occurrence."[25] Thus, coming out to military authorities evoked two entirely different responses, one of which was responsible and productive and the other, irresponsible and destructive.

It should also be noted that once a man formally comes out in the military, it is often difficult to predict exactly how long it will take for his discharge to become effective. Depending upon his command and other factors, including intentional delays on the part of the government, it may only be a few weeks—although it could take up to several months—before he is actually released.

When a gay serviceman contemplates coming out in this context, then, he should be aware that his course may be unpredictable; for this reason, he should not attempt the process alone. Rather, most experts advise that a man in such circumstances seek legal counsel before declaring his sexual orientation to military officials.

Coming Out Privately

In terms of those men who prefer to come out to particular individuals on a confidential basis, they typically choose to tell a close friend, roommate, or co-worker. In many instances, the gay man first opens up to another person whom he believes to be gay, a strategy that is sensible enough, except that in unusual instances it may backfire if the other individual, closeted and fearful of being discovered, reports the incident so as to protect his own secret. Or the gay serviceman may come out to a straight friend whom he trusts, but who subsequently informs the authorities out of a sense of duty or because of a preexisting antagonism toward the gay population. That said, based on the available information, it appears that homosexual men in the military are usually quite careful when determining with whom they will share this information about themselves, such that an individual who is believed to be potentially unreliable is simply not told.

Interestingly, once a homosexual serviceman does open up to another gay person in the armed forces, he may well find himself privy to a network of sorts, an underground system composed of gay service personnel. Just as there are numerous cliques in the military based on common interests and concerns, so too are there gay cliques, groups through which an enlisted man may learn about other homosexual servicemen, as well as about meeting places that are off the military base but still within his area. As a result, he may be better able to socialize with other gay people, share mutual concerns, and develop meaningful relationships. And while a certain degree of risk may be involved in becoming known in such a network, such structures nevertheless serve an important function in that they help the gay serviceman overcome his feelings of isolation and loneliness and assist him in forming authentic, meaningful bonds with others. As it now stands, thousands of enlisted men are currently a part of such networks worldwide.

From the foregoing, it is evident that coming out in the military may be a very different experience than doing so in other types of work settings. Whereas the gay teacher, scientist, or businessman may choose to disclose his orientation to a few trusted co-workers or perhaps more extensively to virtually everyone in the organization, the military man does not have this latter option unless he is willing to give up his job. If he is to come out while retaining his position in the armed forces, then he must do so very carefully and on an individual basis only, not publicly and not officially. Yet even when he comes out privately, he may still be taking a risk, since no legal protections are in place to protect his right to be homosexual. Accordingly, gay servicemen must weigh carefully all of the potential advantages and disadvantages of coming forward and make the decision based on their principles, their needs, and their present and future plans. As well, the larger civilian population must continue to press for formal recognition of the constitutional rights of homosexual men and women to serve in our nation's military, since only when these rights are acknowledged and respected will gay service personnel be in a position to apply themselves fully and without distraction to the responsibilities of their jobs.

CURRENT TRENDS

In this chapter, we have seen that gay men in an array of occupations are coming out in growing numbers. Furthermore, looking ahead it seems likely that this course of events will continue well into the future for at least three interrelated reasons.

First, the current trend toward self-disclosure stems from an enhanced awareness in both the gay and straight populations of the legitimacy of the same-sex orientation, an important basis for social change. Since the 1970s, more and more gay men have come to realize that there is no reason that they should be compelled to hide their sexual dispositions on the job, while a substantial segment of the heterosexual population has at last recognized that it is justifiable to be oriented toward the same gender, that gay workers are as effective as straight ones, and that regardless of individual differences, as citizens of a democracy we must all be afforded the same rights and freedoms. Indeed, as this century has progressed, our society has demonstrated a growing respect for the value and the validity of the diverse groups that compose it, along with a recognition of the fact that these groups are entitled to equal opportunities in the workplace. And in our nation's history, whenever a minority group has come to be viewed in this light, a newfound respect for its rights has typically followed.

Second, because of the burgeoning openness among gay workers today and their demands that their rights be acknowledged and granted, many employers are now instituting formal policies that protect such workers from on-the-job discrimination. Some employers are offering gay couples domestic partner benefits as well, since same-sex relationships are increasingly being recognized as legitimate unions. And still other organizations are requiring that all of their employees undergo "tolerance training," educational programs designed to inform and sensitize workers to various minority groups, including, at times, the gay minority. While most organizations in the United States have not yet instituted antidiscrimination policies that specifically protect gay workers, domestic partner benefits programs, or tolerance training workshops, the fact that the number of those employers that have done so is rising each year bodes well for the future. Such advances make it safer for gay men to come out on the job.

Third, as the same-sex orientation gains greater understanding and acceptance by mainstream society, more men are finding it easier to come out to themselves, to their families and friends, and, by natural progression, to those with whom they work. And as they come forward, these openly gay workers are serving, in many instances, as role models for those new homosexual employees just entering the job market, as well as for older gay employees who joined the workforce during more oppressive times, a sequence of events that contributes to the steady expansion of the openly gay workforce.

It is for these reasons, among others, that the future visibility of gay citizens in the occupation world appears assured.

SUGGESTIONS

In this section, information and advice are offered to the gay man with questions or concerns about coming out on the job, followed by suggestions for heterosexual employers and employees.

1. If you are gay and are considering coming forward in the workplace, first understand that your experience is more likely to be a favorable one if you plan the self-disclosure process in advance and review it as you put it into action. This means being aware of your reasons for coming out at this time and being clear within yourself as to your short-term and long-term goals in doing so. Second, determine how these goals may best be reached; for instance, whether it is advisable to reveal your orientation to one or a few trusted colleagues over the course of time or to disclose it directly to several key people early on in the employment process. Third, try to anticipate any problems that may arise along the way, from personal rejection to company gossip to blatant discrimination, and have in mind reasonable methods of containing such difficulties. And lastly, if there are openly gay employees in your workplace, consider discussing your plans with one or more of them before actually coming out. In this way, you may receive valuable insights and advice applicable to your particular place of employment.

2. Be aware that as an employee who is out of the closet, you may be treated differently than other workers. In some organizations, for instance, the openly gay employee is an easy target for abuse because of his visibility and candor and, perhaps, even considered a special threat because of his strength of character and his forthrightness. Worried that other homosexual workers will follow

his example, those in power may, in exceptional cases, attempt to concoct a pretext by which to either usher him out of the organization or at least silence him in some fashion, such as by transferring him to a more remote location. Or the opposite may occur: being openly gay may protect a worker from maltreatment, since many employers, fearful of sharp legal retaliation, are reluctant to engage in any sort of action that might be construed as discriminatory against an employee who is a member of a recognized minority group.

At the present time, gay workers in a growing number of settings are shielded from on-the-job abuse by means of nondiscrimination policies that include sexual orientation as an identified characteristic. While high-tech corporations led in this advance, policies formally protecting gay workers from unfair treatment can now be found at many colleges and universities, in the entertainment and service industries, and in certain federal, state, and municipal settings. Of course, carefully orchestrated discrimination can occur in such a way as to obscure its true nature, the result being that policies for its prevention may have only limited effectiveness. But the fact that sexual orientation is now being judged as irrelevant to job performance and that legal efforts are being made to protect the gay citizenry in this regard is heartening.

In your own case, if you are considering coming out on the job, it would be advisable for you to learn in advance what, if any, protections your workplace offers in the event that your disclosure leads to mistreatment. To this end, you might contact the personnel department at your workplace or check with the appropriate municipal, state, or federal office if you are employed by the government.

3. If you are heterosexual, try to understand and appreciate the situation of gay workers. By placing yourself in their circumstances, you may better grasp the range of impediments that they so often face. For instance, the majority of gay men do not acknowledge their same-sex orientations on the job, which means that they also do not discuss their life partners or any other aspects of their lives that might reveal their sexual dispositions. As a heterosexual, consider for a moment the difficulty of never mentioning to your colleagues that you are married or providing any other information that might point to the fact that you have a partner, as well as

censoring at all times any details of your personal life that might indicate that you are straight. Or imagine mentioning casually on the job that you do have a partner of the opposite sex or some other feature of your life that indicates that you are heterosexual, then suffering ostracism, mockery, and perhaps job discrimination as a consequence. This is what worklife can be like for a gay employee in certain settings.

To help counter such injustice, you might choose to serve as a role model for your heterosexual co-workers or employees. If gay workers are disparaged in your workplace, for instance, stand up for them, support them, and encourage straight workers to do likewise. As well, demonstrate an unwavering fairness in your interactions with gay workers so that others might learn from your example. It is in such ways, through both gay and straight people striving to eliminate prejudice in the workplace, that all workers ultimately benefit since the eventual result is a more mature, diverse, and humane environment for everyone.

Chapter 4

The Public Sphere:
Managing Widespread Exposure

The final departure from the closet, for at least some gay men, occurs when they come forward on a scale that is vast and irrevocable; namely, at a highly visible, public level. This may be the case, for instance, for the politician who feels it important that his constituency understand that he has a same-sex orientation or for the filmmaker or professional athlete whose social conscience impels him to use his standing in the public eye to illustrate that gay citizens, like straight ones, hold positions of accomplishment and influence in society. But before we embark on a discussion of such progressive individuals and of their actions to advance the gay population as a whole, let us first turn our attention to the person whose homosexuality becomes known publicly, but against his will, his orientation being exposed by others for political reasons or by the individual himself engaging in acts that inadvertently bring into wide view his sexual nature.

THE PUBLIC CRUCIBLE

In the preceding chapters, we have seen that the coming-out experience is a complex psychological journey that may take years to complete if, indeed, it is ever truly completed. We have seen, as well, that while there exist identifiable stages through which many people pass as they come forward, the process itself remains a deeply personal one. This is because each of us navigates his own way through an array of influences, from our unique childhood experiences and early concepts of homosexuality to our current employment circumstances and plans for the future. It follows, then, that the coming-out experience, because it typically involves the emergence of highly charged, and inherently private, emotional and familial issues, may be seriously derailed if a person is not granted the freedom and dignity to come forward naturally, but instead hurled prematurely into public view as a "closet homosexual" by overzealous activists or by untimely events. And, unfortunately, in a society that is all too often derelict in acknowledging and respecting its members' emotional well-being, not to mention their rights to privacy, it does happen that a gay man's sexual orientation may, at times, be cast into the harsh glare of public recognition at an inordinately high cost to the man himself.

OUTING AND ITS EFFECTS

A striking example of such exposure can be found in the practice of *outing*. Beginning, in part, with media interviews with novelist Armistead Maupin in the 1980s—interviews in which he "named names"—and continuing into the early 1990s, a handful of journalists, gossip columnists among them, sought to introduce into common practice a tactic by which presumably closeted public figures were to be exposed as homosexual by the media and thus held up to public scrutiny. But whereas in former times, most notably during the McCarthy era, such incidents of gay citizens being publicly branded in this manner were engineered by intolerant heterosexuals bent on destroying the careers, if not the lives, of gay men and women, the recent resurrection of this practice has been perpetrated by self-identified gay people themselves, most often by gay men.

Since it is not our purpose here to review the entire history and course of this controversial affair, the interested reader is referred to that body of literature that exists elsewhere on the subject. Suffice it to say, however, the recent trend toward outing does not enjoy the favor of the majority of men and women, gay or straight, nor that of the mainstream press, which has steadfastly refused to adopt it as a standard journalistic practice. Instead, the prevailing opinion continues to be the traditional one: a person's sexual orientation and intimate behavior are personal information; therefore, it is the individual's choice if, when, and to whom he discloses it.

Steve Barbone and Lee Rice of Marquette University write the following:

[W]e can and should be able to conceal our sexual orientation for the same reason we conceal our bank accounts, our lovers' tastes in food, or a myriad of other information, not because the *content* of the information is a source of shame (to us), but rather because our interlocutor does not enjoy a level of access which makes such information appropriate.[1]

We should note, as well, that this controversial move toward outing seems to be winding down somewhat, which is not surprising given that the method has serious limitations. Among its principal drawbacks is the fact that publicly baring an individual's sexual disposition produces few, if any, benefits either for the person or for society at large, such that the practice cannot reasonably be expected to succeed as an instrument of social change. At most, it serves a punitive role by stripping power from a closeted homosexual person considered to be against gay political interests, a seldom-acknowledged motive. Nevertheless, because episodes of outing still occur on occasion and because these acts do represent a dramatic short-circuiting of the coming-out process, it should serve us well to review briefly the claims and consequences of this form of public exposure.

Rationales and Rationalizations

As it stands, many of those who are opposed to outing consider the practice to be nothing more than a thinly-veiled attempt by the gay radical fringe to publicly thrash well-known individuals who have not come forward sufficiently to please them. Those who support outing, on the other hand, offer certain justifications for their beliefs. Among their chief claims are that such exposure (1) provides highly visible, even famous, role models for gay youth, (2) illustrates to the mainstream population that there exist distinguished men and women who are homosexual and who hold positions of value and esteem in society, and (3) impels closeted public figures to recognize and fulfill their obligations to work for the betterment of the gay community. Despite the social value suggested by these claims, however, a close inspection reveals fundamental flaws in the claims themselves.

It is evident, for instance, that a person who is forcibly revealed as gay is not a suitable role model for young people; if he must be evicted from the closet, then he is no exemplar for anyone. Moreover, when activists offer up a peer to mainstream society in this manner, the straight population is nearly always disdainful; the gay community is perceived as not only violating its members' privacy, but, worse still, cannibalizing its own as a sacrifice for anticipated political gain. And indeed, the exposed person usually suffers greatly because of the ordeal, in a fall from grace that ironically causes him to lose much, if not all, of the power and influence for which he was supposedly spotlighted in the first place. And the argument that outing encourages a closeted public figure to acknowledge and fulfill a fundamental obligation to the gay citizenry is based on the premise that the person, by virtue of the fact that he is homosexual, is accountable to the gay community and must work on its behalf, a debatable assertion in that the concept of choice is excluded from consideration. The reality is, most of those who have been the targets of outings have felt no such allegiance to the gay community, nor have they subsequently worked for its benefit. Some have not even considered themselves to be gay, either because they are not—they are bisexual or perhaps heterosexual, like former Speaker of the House Tom Foley, whose sexual orientation was slyly misrepresented by the Republican National Committee—or they are homosexual but have not yet come to terms with the fact and thus lack a stable gay identity. This brings us to a salient point about the process of sexual self-disclosure and about the untenable basis of outing as an act of genuine revelation.

Sexual Orientation versus Sexual Identity

When we speak of the coming-out experience, we are referring to a process that begins internally and, over the course of time, manifests itself externally, a process of soul searching and self-discovery that culminates in the development of a gay identity, an identity that one eventually reveals to others. Of course, human nature being what it is—inquisitive, impulsive, and insensitive at times—other people in the individual's life may, long before he has had the opportunity to complete this inner odyssey, speculate on his erotic disposition and among themselves conclude that he is homosexual.

In actuality, however, only one person is in the position to state unequivocally that the man is indeed gay, at least in terms of his self-definition, and that is the man himself. Being an internal construct, his sexual identity must issue from within him; it cannot be assigned to him by others. It is therefore important that we distinguish between an individual's sexual orientation and his sexual identity when we announce that he is gay, since the two may be at odds, as is frequently the case in the early stages of the coming-out process.

Indeed, as we noted in Chapter 1, a person who is homosexual may at first consider himself to be heterosexual or bisexual, despite the existence of persistent same-sex urges. Having been raised to think of himself as straight, he finds that he must struggle to reconcile his long-standing heterosexual image of himself with his newly discovered homosexual needs, a lengthy and painstaking process during which he may, for a certain period of time, persist in viewing himself as nongay even as he forges affectional and sexual bonds with other males. Consequently, if during this period the individual were to be labeled publicly as homosexual, the inner conflict that he had been striving to resolve might well intensify to the point of damaging him emotionally, arresting the natural unfolding of the coming-out process while punishing him bitterly through public humiliation. Not surprisingly, exposures of this sort, because they thrust a person's most private and sensitive identity issues into the public eye, often have devastating consequences.

Effects of Involuntary Public Exposure

When a newspaper in Tennessee, for instance, published a series of articles—at least eight of them, by one account[2]—identifying local men who had been arrested for allegedly engaging in sex in public places, one of those named, a university professor, killed himself. And while the newspaper refused to accept any responsibility for this man's emotional reaction and subsequent death, it is quite possible that the gentleman would not have committed suicide had such information about him not been publicized by the media. The fact is, all too often those who consider it their duty to reveal to the public the sexual deeds of the citizenry fail to recognize their own role in the hardships these individuals subsequently suffer, including the onset of inner turmoil that may be intense, long-lasting, and, in many cases, disabling.

Guilt and Shame

The gay youth or adult who is struggling with the moral and ethical dimensions of his sexual disposition, for instance, and who, for this reason, has not yet come out of the closet may be horrified to find that he has been thrust into public view as homosexual. Such a broad exposure may be his cardinal fear, a harrowing prospect to which he is exquisitely sensitive. As a result, he may not only be stunned by the sudden, widespread attention to his sexuality, but overwhelmed as well by powerful and pervasive feelings of guilt; guilt simply for having loved, and perhaps made love to, other males. At such a moment, self-reproach washes over him because he has not progressed beyond that early stage in the coming-out process when he subscribes to the notion that his sexual feelings are abnormal or immoral.

Even more fundamentally, an abrupt public exposure of this sort may induce in him a resounding sense of shame—a wholesale dismissal of himself as a bad or unworthy person—in addition to his feelings of guilt, which are usually linked more specifically to his sexual behavior itself. And shame emerges because the ordeal is played out in the public arena. Being dragged unceremoniously out of the shadows and held up for inspection by an entire community can certainly make one feel disgraced. In fact, such an event is but a modern-day reenactment of the ancient ritual of accusation, judgment, and condemnation by the tribe, the damnation of the individual and the demand for atonement, a mortifying ordeal.

"The phenomenological experience of the person having shame is that of a wish to hide, disappear, and die," writes Michael Lewis, professor of pediatrics, psychiatry, and psychology at the Robert Wood Johnson Medical School and author of the book *Shame: The Exposed Self*.[3] "This emotional state is so intense and has such a devastating effect on the self-system that individuals presented with such a state must attempt to rid themselves of it. However, since shame represents a global attack on the self, people have great difficulty in dissipating this emotion."

A form of self-rejection, shame emerges when one judges his value as a human being to be uncommonly low, based on the reactions he receives about himself from those around him. In the case of outing, a substantial number of people may treat the person like a pariah once they discover that he has concealed his homosexuality. Along with the negative reactions of the public at large, heterosexual family members, friends, and co-workers may no longer wish to associate with him because they feel uneasy with his sexual disposition, while openly gay acquaintances may shun him because of what they regard, correctly or incorrectly, as his secretive, misleading past. Consequently, the person may find himself spiraling into an emotional and spiritual abyss and in dire need of support, yet rebuffed by straight and gay people alike, a dismaying turn of events that may leave him feeling banished. Thus alienated and ashamed, he may conclude that such treatment indicates beyond doubt that he is a worthless person, a grave misreading of the events that may influence him for years to come. Certainly such a conclusion may make it extremely difficult for the person to regain his self-respect, as well as reestablish the coming-out process and develop a realistic, healthy view of his sexuality. Instead, he thereafter may remain reluctant to express openly his sexual orientation due to the deep-seated conviction, however unlikely, that dreadful repercussions will surely follow if he does.

Identity Confusion

In addition, accompanying such feelings of guilt and shame may be a profound sense of confusion. Now that he has been portrayed in public as a "closet case," those who are important in the person's life may regard him as having been deceitful to them in the past and thus as untrustworthy in the present. Yet the individual may not see himself in this way at all, especially since his intention might never have been to mislead anyone. At the stage in the coming-out process during which he was captured in the public eye, he may have genuinely believed himself to be largely nongay, having not yet realized the truth of the matter. But because others now behave toward him as if his integrity is suspect, in his pain and confusion the individual himself may begin to doubt his own character.

He may experience immense confusion, too, about his sexual orientation itself, as we have already noted, with such an abrupt exposure creating what has been described elsewhere as an "obstruction in consolidating a gay identity."[4] If, for instance, the person were unsure of, or conflicted about, his sexual nature when he was outed, then he would likely feel deeply confounded when other people proclaim that he is gay, since this outsider's view of his inner world would be at odds with his own understanding of his affectional nature. And while such a public perception is typically upsetting to the person who has not yet determined that he has a same-sex orientation, to the homosexual individual who is nearer to the truth, and therefore less able to use denial as a defense against it, the revelation may be deeply traumatic in that it may prompt him to realize prematurely that he is gay. By forcing him to face his sexual disposition before he is equipped to do so, the natural process of self-discovery through which he otherwise might have evolved into a healthy, openly gay man is aborted and, in its place, a blunt sexual awareness is triggered within him that he may be incapable of integrating into his personality. The result may be lasting psychological damage.

Life Consequences

Of course, compounding such complex inner problems may be the real-life aftermath of the exposure itself. Above and beyond the social shaming of the individual, other people may act in ways that directly, and detrimentally, affect his life itself.

"The violation of privacy involved in outing someone is—or at least very much like—theft," say David Mayo and Martin Gunderson.[5] "It is theft from that person of control of private information. When someone loses control of that information, he or she may very well suffer serious harm, especially if that information triggers responses of prejudice, intolerance, and malice in others." And, indeed, such harm does occur at times.

Partly as a result of the damaging attitudes and conduct of other people, for instance, the individual who is outed may face profound losses, including the loss of his job, his income, his future employability, and perhaps his wife and children if he is married. And given that the person may already be struggling with a sense of confusion and feelings of humiliation and isolation, the added toll of such elemental losses may cause him to lapse further into a depressed state, thus rendering it even more difficult for him to manage the escalating crisis.

The dramatic downfall of Robert Bauman, a former Republican member of the U.S. House of Representatives, illustrates both the emotional reactions and the professional ruination that may occur when one is brusquely called to account, in public, for his homosexual activities. A married Roman Catholic with four children, this ultraconservative congressman, having something of a national reputation for being intensely antigay in his legislative role, was accused by federal investigators of soliciting sex from an underage male prostitute. Naturally, this allegation unleashed a feeding frenzy among the media since the charge contained all the ingredients of a grand scandal: homosexual misconduct with a minor, adultery, and hypocrisy by a government official. For Mr. Bauman, however, the accusation led to a state of shock, withdrawal, depression, and, at one point, thoughts of self-destruction.[6] He wrote the following:

> At such times, the mind tends to extremes and I had indeed considered suicide. Driving home the night before my court appearance . . . I gazed down at the dark waters of Chesapeake as we crossed the Bay Bridge near Annapolis. It would have been so easy to just end it all. But then I thought, "Why give the bastards the satisfaction?"[7]

Although the former right-wing leader decided to go on with his life and overcome, as much as possible, the obstacles confronting him, the losses were severe: his marriage collapsed, his congressional career came to an end, and new employment became difficult for him to secure, a snowballing of consequences that no doubt complicated the coping process. And that is the point: an array of losses that command one's attention and demand a resolution may occur suddenly and cumulatively during such ordeals, especially in those instances in which a person's self-presentation in public is in striking contrast to his private behavior.

Such was the case for Rock Hudson, a man whose public persona and private life were profoundly discrepant and who was outed by the *San Francisco Chronicle* in 1985 after he developed AIDS. If

there was a political motive behind the exposure of Hudson's homosexuality, an aspect of his life that both the actor and the studios
guarded scrupulously for decades, it may have been to publicize the
fact that an American film legend could contract the virus. To be
sure, until this story broke, the epidemic had been largely overlooked
by the Reagan administration, the media, and the mainstream population. Still, the incident raises serious questions about the media's
responsibility not only to the public at large, but to the individual
who is the subject of its reports.

"With on-the-record quotes from a circle of Hudson's longtime
friends in San Francisco," writes Randy Shilts in the AIDS chronicle, *And the Band Played On*, "the story discussed the torment of a
man who had for years struggled with the question of whether he
might do some good by acknowledging his sexuality."[8] Yet, the
decision to come out publicly was not one that Hudson was permitted to make; rather, a newspaper made it for him while he was in
the grip of a life-threatening condition. As for the impact this convoluted turn of events may have had on the actor during his last
months of life, because he was largely secluded during this time, it
remains unknown.

Still, in all fairness, it should be noted that not all outings have
distressing outcomes for the individuals so targeted. In a small number of instances, the long-range effects may even be somewhat beneficial. In this regard, it appears that the person who is emotionally
mature, unmarried, and far enough along in the coming-out process
to have begun constructing for himself a positive gay identity may be
in a much better position to shoulder such an intrusive assault than
the married man who remains uncertain of his sexual orientation.

Consider, for instance, former Congressman Gerry Studds of Massachusetts. A liberal representative, Studds, prior to being revealed
as gay was, by many accounts, well along in the coming-out process. For this and other reasons, he seemed to adjust readily to
media reports about his same-sex orientation and his purported
relationship with a young male page on Capitol Hill. In fact, the
congressman went so far as to declare in a subsequent interview
with the gay press that, now that he was officially out of the closet,
he felt better than at any other point in his life.[9] As for his political
career, Studds continued to be elected to office after the exposure.

It would appear, then, that being outed may, in selected cases, help a person become more admissibly gay, something he might not have been willing or able to do otherwise. Nevertheless, we must bear in mind that while productive outcomes of this sort do take place on occasion and are certainly heartening when they occur, they remain the exception. Traumatic reactions continue to be the rule.

The fact is, the coming-out process is a lengthy, intricate undertaking and, as such, may be undermined if other people, for political or other reasons, reveal to the public an individual's sexual orientation and intimate practices before he is prepared for such sweeping visibility. As we have seen, an act of this magnitude, besides potentially impairing the person's mental and spiritual health, may lead to tangible losses in his life, losses that may be both profound and irreversible. And while such devastation may not occur in all cases, it would certainly seem to happen frequently enough to warrant a serious review of the practice. The reality is that most of those who are in the closet are there for a reason: either they have not yet resolved within themselves the inner conflicts that emerge as one realizes that he is homosexual, or they consider their surroundings to be hostile to, and therefore unsafe for, openly gay people.

Accordingly, if we are to grant each member of the gay citizenry the respect that he deserves—regardless of the point at which he happens to be in the coming-out process or the relative safety or danger of his immediate environment—then a case can be made that the practice of involuntary exposure should be halted. Except in the most extenuating of circumstances, the consequences of outing, including its psychological effects, are too potentially damaging for it to be considered an acceptable act. Instead, if an individual is to become known as homosexual at the public level, then such exposure should be initiated by the person himself and should represent his own wishes, with the disclosure itself being prepared carefully in advance and delivered in such a manner as to reflect favorably on both the gay person and the gay population. In this way, not only is no one harmed, but together the individual and society share the benefits of his revelation; a profitable approach, and an alternative to outing that is morally defensible, politically pragmatic, and personally empowering.

THE DECISION TO GO PUBLIC

Empowerment is also a principal reason that a growing number of people today, including well-known figures in an array of professions, are *choosing* to identify themselves as gay in the public realm, many times against the counsel of concerned family, friends, and colleagues. From former NFL linebacker Dave Kopay in the 1970s to U.S. Army Soldier of the Year Joe Zuniga in the 1990s, more and more men are making their same-sex orientations known to the mainstream population in order to fortify themselves and to bolster the gay community. And indeed, such broad visibility often serves an important psychological function for the individual, confirming his sense of personal integrity and legitimizing his sexual identity, while advancing the interests of the gay population itself. That said, it should be noted that most gay men who are otherwise out of the closet do not go on to reveal their sexual orientations in the public arena, either because they believe that they lack the opportunity to do so in a significant manner or because they are uncomfortable politicizing their sexuality in this way, concerned that it transforms what should be, in their opinion, a personal aspect of their lives into a public product. Of course, in many cases, fear is the real reason, fear of the negative fallout to which they and their loved ones might be subjected were they to come forward to such a marked degree. In any event, in the next section we look at those gay individuals who, despite the potential risks involved, do decide to come out at the public level and at the effects that such heightened visibility has on their lives.

Reasons for Coming Out

During the past two decades, one phenomenon, more than any other, has prompted countless men to reveal their same-sex orientations in public settings: the HIV epidemic. Because of this staggering health crisis, thousands of men, having developed noticeable symptoms of the disease, have found themselves in the awkward position of having to deal with uninvited public attention both to their medical conditions and to their presumed homosexuality. Certainly, being relatively young and unmarried and displaying visible signs of HIV disease can render one vulnerable to gossip and innuendo, while the demands of the condition itself can make it imperative that one discuss the matter with those central to his life. Not surprisingly, then, men in such straits have sometimes felt outed by the virus. More to the point, once they have come out in this way, a certain portion of them have gone on to become prominent AIDS activists, publicizing their medical conditions and their same-sex orientations as they press for enhanced education, research, and treatment of the syndrome.

In other cases, men who do not harbor the virus have also come out publicly because of their involvement in the epidemic, usually while assisting those who are infected. Typically, they have permitted their sexual dispositions to become widely known or assumed through their work with AIDS service organizations perceived to be predominantly gay. Of course, like some of those who are infected, a certain portion have chosen to go even further, publicizing their same-sex orientations so that they might use the attendant visibility to inform the mainstream population about HIV disease and its tragic, and unacceptable, impact on the gay citizenry. Some of them have even attained national or international renown as writers, speakers, or lobbyists as a result of their efforts.

Larry Kramer, for instance, although already established as a gay playwright and film producer prior to the advent of the AIDS crisis, became even more prominent early in the epidemic when he began calling attention to, and demanding action against, the epidemic's encroachment into the gay community. Among other things, he cofounded the Gay Men's Health Crisis, as well as making his political opinions known through a series of controversial essays. He also encouraged gay men to come out publicly in order to challenge what he perceived as the government's indolence in the face of this thundering epidemic:

> I am sick of closeted gays. There is only one thing that's going to save some of us, and that is *numbers* and pressure and our being perceived as united and a threat. . . . Unless we can generate, visibly, numbers, masses, we are going to die.[10]

To AIDS activists like Larry Kramer, then, coming out is viewed as part of a larger humanitarian and political strategy to ensure the survival of the gay population itself. Of course, other activists, even before the HIV epidemic, foresaw the advantages of large numbers of gay citizens coming forward publicly, among them politician Harvey Milk.

Born and reared on Long Island and the son of a businessman, Milk was apparently not forthcoming about his same-sex orientation during most of his adult life, at least not to any meaningful degree. But once he moved to Castro Street in San Francisco in the 1970s and, as a businessman himself, became dissatisfied with several aspects of that city's political machine, he developed a taste for the political process and eventually ran for office as a homosexual candidate. After three defeats, Milk surged ahead of seventeen other candidates to win a seat on the Board of Supervisors and become, in 1977, the first openly gay city official in American history.

In terms of being an *out* public figure, Milk persistently used his position to implore gay San Franciscans—indeed, all of gay America—to come further out of the closet. Throughout his incumbency, he viewed such forthrightness as being beneficial both to the individual, in that it was a powerful act of self-affirmation, and to the collective, since it was a tool through which the gay citizenry could dismantle the myths that undermined it and secure the rights to which it is entitled.

"A gay person in office can set a tone," said Milk, referring to the need for a gay presence in government.[11] "(He) can command respect not only from the larger community, but from the young people in our own community who need both examples and hope."

As for the homosexual citizenry itself, Milk said the following:

> I would like to see every gay lawyer, every gay architect come out, stand up and let the world know. That would do more to end prejudice overnight than anybody could imagine. I urge them to do that, urge them to come out. Only that way will we start to achieve our rights.[12]

Openly gay when he entered office, then, Harvey Milk used his visibility and authority to address the needs of his largely gay constituency, while also attending conscientiously to the needs of the other groups that composed his district. In this respect, he followed a path similar to that of Elaine Noble, a woman who, a few years earlier on the other side of the nation, became the first publicly acknowledged gay person to be elected to office at the state level.

Noble initially came out in 1970 while seeking a teaching position at Emerson College. Finding no compelling reason to mislead the institution about her sexual orientation—and assuming that the students would probably figure out that she was gay anyway—Noble disclosed it to school officials prior to accepting a position.[13] Then, four years later, she ran for a seat in the Massachusetts House of Representatives as an openly gay candidate and won. In the years that followed, Noble also won well-deserved respect as a representative who faithfully served all of her consituency's interests, as well as praise for her efforts to introduce legislation protecting gay citizens from discrimination.

Of course, there have been others who likewise came out under relatively insulated conditions and went on to become well-known gay public figures, among them Czechoslovakian-born tennis champion Martina Navratilova, who disclosed her sexual disposition to officials of the Immigration and Naturalization Service and later to New York's *Daily News*,[14] and Margarethe Cammermeyer, a colonel and Chief Nurse of the Washington National Guard who came out during a routine interview to obtain a security clearance.

Cammermeyer, a mother of four, had been a nurse in Vietnam and had helped establish the state's National Guard hospital. By all accounts, she was an extraordinary woman. In fact, at the time of her interview, she was fulfilling both civilian and reservist duties while pursuing doctoral studies with aspirations of becoming a general and the Chief Nurse at the national level. To this end, she was seeking a clearance so that she could attend the War College, a prerequisite for advancement. By answering, "I am a lesbian," when asked about her personal life, however, Cammermeyer unwittingly sparked a chain of events that culminated in her discharge from the service. "If they could do this to me," she asked, "what were they doing to others who had less rank and visibility?"[15]

Although she subsequently challenged the expulsion, the military prevailed. Nevertheless, sensitized to the extent of the armed forces' inequitable stance on homosexuality, Cammermeyer thereafter used her newly established public persona to draw attention to the flaws in its policy. "I hoped people would listen to my message," she said, "and I could speak for those less visible."[16] Thus, while she initially disclosed her sexuality to an interviewer in the course of a seemingly personal discussion, Cammermeyer eventually came out at the national level so that she could continue contesting, in the public eye, the unjust practices of a highly rigid institution.

In a similar vein, Air Force Technical Sergeant Leonard Matlovich officially revealed his homosexuality in order to challenge the military's exclusionary position, but, from the beginning, with the intention of contesting the policy's constitutionality at the level of the Supreme Court. Unlike Cammermeyer, he did not come out during a routine, one-to-one interview, nor was it discovered by others; rather, he submitted it in writing to his commanding officer in a deliberate effort to throw down the gauntlet on behalf of all gay service personnel.[17]

A race relations instructor in the military, Matlovich had served three tours of duty in Vietnam, been awarded numerous awards, including the Bronze Star and the Purple Heart, and was the highest noncommissioned officer teaching race relations in the Tactical Air Command. His record was impeccable. In terms of his sexual unfolding, however, it was not nearly as smooth, with the sergeant being largely unaware of his true sexual nature for a substantial part of his adult life. When, at last, he did determine that he was gay, however, he also awakened to the prospect of discrimination that he and other gay service personnel faced. Indeed, prejudice had been the basis of the race relations classes he had been teaching. As a result, his sense of justice obliged him to come out publicly.

"It was getting to the point I couldn't live with myself," he said.[18] "I began to feel that I was a coward inside because I wasn't willing to do what I was telling other people to do. . . . I felt two-faced."

Accordingly, Matlovich informed the military that he was homosexual, received a discharge, then challenged the action in court and won. But because the military was expected to appeal the decision and to win on appeal, Matlovich ultimately dropped his challenge, accepted a monetary settlement, and returned to civilian life. Still, the former sergeant continued to travel the nation as an openly gay speaker, lecturing to groups both large and small about the military's discriminatory policies and about the necessity of coming out.

"I think everyone must leave the closet sometime," he said.[19] "I'm not the person to harm those who are not ready by dragging them out, but I think they are hurting us all by not coming forward."

Thus, Leonard Matlovich, like the others we have discussed here, recognized the importance of being candid about his sexual disposition. He understood that visibility is crucial to bringing about social change, since it is through such a presence that we may finally correct the mainstream population's distorted images of the gay citizenry.

Supporting Data

In this regard, it should be noted that recent studies by Gregory Herek and his associates lend support to this notion.[20] These researchers surveyed 538 heterosexual adults and found that those who knew at least one gay individual on a personal basis were much more likely to hold favorable opinions of the gay population as a whole than were those who had no prior contact with a homosexual person. Moreover, they found that those who knew a larger number of gay men and women were inclined to report even more positive views of the gay citizenry. And these are not the only investigations to have yielded such findings.

Says Herek, referring to nine additional studies, "Survey research . . . has consistently shown that heterosexuals who report personal contact with gay men and lesbians express significantly more favorable attitudes toward gay people as a group than do heterosexuals who lack contact experiences."[21] And such findings, he contends, support the contact hypothesis, which holds that, under given conditions, direct involvement and, thus, greater familiarity between members of estranged social groups promotes a more peaceful coexistence.[22] Accordingly, the argument put forth by many gay public figures—namely, that increased visibility is a viable strategy for gaining social acceptance and, hence, social advancement—appears to be a valid one.

Repercussions

In terms of the aftermath of coming out publicly, as one might expect, a spectrum of results may follow. And while positive outcomes certainly occur, at times the repercussions are more negative, most often when the gay person is in a position to bring about significant change in society, since he may be viewed as a threat to the status quo. For that matter, anyone in a highly influential position, regardless of his sexual nature, may be vulnerable to harsh counteractions if he works for social or political reform, as the histories of Mahatma Gandhi, Martin Luther King Jr., Robert Kennedy, and Anwar Sadat attest.

Regarding those public figures we have discussed in this chapter, after Leonard Matlovich announced that he was gay and proceeded to contest the military's policy, adversaries shot at his house. He also received phone threats and was excommunicated by the Mormon Church.[23] Elaine Noble likewise had her house fired upon, her car tampered with, and threats phoned to her. A car belonging to one her of campaign workers was bombed, and a local Catholic priest, in an act corroding the boundary between church and state, threatened to excommunicate anyone who voted for her.[24] And Harvey Milk was assassinated.

By comparison, gay public figures who are considered less likely to bring about significant change are not nearly as vulnerable to such violence. Homosexual sports figures, for instance, rarely report such incidents, although they may suffer milder discrimination in the form of receiving few, if any, offers to endorse commercial products and the like. And openly gay entertainment figures, because they are not considered agents of social or political reform, are less prone to volatile reactions from the public.

Another important factor is the historical moment at which the person decides to publicly come out. To do so in the 1960s was to guarantee repudiation, except perhaps for those in a handful of professions, such as the arts. In the 1970s, however, a decade marked by an enhanced tolerance of gays and lesbians, coming forward publicly more often met with favor, as it did during the 1980s until the HIV epidemic brought a wave of antigay hysteria. Today, the social climate has again become relatively accepting of homosexual public figures, with negative repercussions, on the whole, being less likely than in the past.

Comparing the experiences of selected individuals, we can see the progress. When Dave Kopay, the former NFL running back, came out in 1976, he was ostracized by certain segments of the population for doing so, yet when Greg Louganis, the Olympic diver, came forward in the 1990s, he received a tremendous surge of support from the mainstream population, along with a TV movie deal. And while openly gay political figures in the 1970s, such as Harvey Milk, at times caught heat because of their same-sex orientations, gay politicians in more recent times, such as Barney Frank, have enjoyed the admiration of the public, in part because of their accessibility as gay men.

Barney Frank is a distinguished member of the House of Representatives from the Commonwealth of Massachusetts who was first elected to public office in 1972. At that early date, he withheld from the public his sexual orientation because, by his own account, he wanted to win elections.[25] He reasoned that if he were to launch his political career as an openly homosexual candidate, he could expect a very short-lived career.

By 1986, however, Representative Frank had resolved to come out publicly, which he did the following year in a *Boston Globe* interview. He then went on to become the most visible gay politician in the nation. At the present time, he continues to be elected to office and remains a staunch supporter of legislation to secure the rights of the gay and lesbian citizenry.

Recently I asked Representative Frank if, in retrospect, acknowledging his sexual orientation at the public level had been the right decision for him. I was particularly interested in its long-term impact on his personal life and congressional career. His response, which is recounted in the foreword, touches on many of the points made throughout this book and is a heartening statement of value to anyone who may be considering coming out at the public level.[26]

From the foreword, it is evident that Representative Frank, like several others we have discussed, with time and experience evolved to the point at which he sought complete visibility as a gay man, an act that proved very valuable in several important respects. It is hoped that, in the years ahead, many more men and women will be encouraged by examples of this sort and will likewise come forward publicly when it is feasible to do so. To be sure, it is through such a heightened visibility that we, as gay citizens, place ourselves in the best position to demonstrate to the world our significant presence, our rich diversity, and our inherent humanity as a people.

SUGGESTIONS

If you are considering coming out in the public sphere, be aware that once you do, the revelation may well be irreversible; that by going on record as gay, this may be how you will be known there-after by most, if not all, people. While this is usually what one desires when he seeks such a high degree of visibility, you should be sensitive to the fact that certain difficulties may accompany it at times. Of course, those who come forward publicly are usually well aware of the potential risks and feel confident that they can manage them.

Bear in mind, too, that some people, particularly those who do not know you well, may thereafter see you less as an individual and more as a representative of a sexual orientation, defining you in terms that are more erotically tinged than would be the case if you were thought to be heterosexual. Others may assume, too, that you are more liberal or bohemian or militant than is actually the case, simply because certain segments of the population still catalogue openly gay men in such ways. For this reason, you may need to exercise patience with, and be prepared to help educate, those you may encounter along the way who have misunderstandings about what it means to be gay.

Of course, it is also important that you appreciate the far-reaching benefits that coming out publicly may bring to you. First of all, by coming forward, you eliminate the possibility of being outed or otherwise having your sexual orientation used against you. Rather, you place yourself in a position whereby you can conduct your life confidently and forthrightly in all its dimensions. By being frank about your sexual orientation, you also free yourself to speak out publicly on matters of relevance to the homosexual citizenry. And as an openly gay person, you may serve as a role model for gay youth at a time when such exemplars are most assuredly needed. Thus, by coming forward in such an expansive fashion, you may experience not only a heightened sense of integrity and self-respect, but also a distinct increase in the value of your life itself in that your public visibility may, in its own way, contribute to the advancement of the gay population as a whole. And this is reason for pride.

Appendix

Coming-Out Resources

Provided in this listing is a variety of gay-related resources in the areas of the family, the workplace, HIV prevention and treatment, and legal and religious issues. Locations include both on-line and street addresses.

THE FAMILY

Youth

Gayteen
http://www.youth.org/gayteen

Youth Assistance Organization (on-line help for gay youth)
http://youth.org

Coalition for Positive Sexuality: Just Say Yes (safer sex guide for teens)
http://www.positive.org/cps

Teens Teaching AIDS Prevention
1-800-234-TEEN

National Gay Youth Network
Post Office Box 846
San Francisco, California 94101

National Coalition of Gay, Lesbian, and Bisexual Youth
Post Office Box 24589
San Jose, California 95154

International Gay and Lesbian Youth Organization
Post Office Box 42463
Washington, DC 20015
http://qrd.tcp.com/qrd/orgs/IGLYO

Adult

"My Child is GAY! Now What Do I Do?"
http://www.pe.net/~bidstrup/parents.htm

Straight Spouse Support Network
http://qrd.tcp.com/qrd/www/orgs/sssn/home.htm

Gay Fathers Coalition
Post Office Box 19891
Washington, DC 20036

Gay and Lesbian Parents Coalition International
Post Office Box 50360
Washington, DC 20091
http://qrd.tcp.com/qrd/www/orgs/glpci/index.html

Parents and Friends of Lesbians and Gays (PFLAG)
1012 14th Street, NW Suite 700
Washington, DC 20005
http://www.pflag.org

THE WORKPLACE

Gay Workplace Issues
http://www.nyu.edu/pages/sls/gaywork

American Civil Liberties Union (ACLU): Workplace Rights
http://www.aclu.org/issues/worker/hmwr.html

High Tech Gays
http://www.htg.org

Servicemembers' Legal Defense Network (military)
http://www.sldn.org

LEGAL: Law Enforcement Gays and Lebians International
http://users.aol.com/legalmn2/Legal-I.html

Gay, Lesbian, and Straight Teachers Network
http://www.glstn.org/freedom

**National Education Association, Division of Human
and Civil Rights**
1201 16th Street, NW
Washington, DC 20036
http://www.nea.org

**National Organization of Gay and Lesbian Scientists
and Technicians**
Post Office Box 91803
Pasadena, California 91109
http://qrd.tcp.com/qrd/orgs/NOGLSTP

National Lesbian and Gay Law Association
Post Office Box 77130
Washington, DC 20013
http://www.nlgla.org

Gay and Lesbian Medical Association
273 Church Street
San Francisco, California 94114
http://www.glma.org

National Gay and Lesbian Nurses
208 W. 13th Street
New York, New York 10011

National Association of Social Workers (Gay and Lesbian)
7981 Eastern Avenue
Silver Spring, Maryland 20910

HIV PREVENTION AND TREATMENT

AIDS Virtual Library
http://planetq.com/aidsvl/index.html

Centers for Disease Control and Prevention (CDC)
National AIDS Clearinghouse
National AIDS Hotline: 1-800-342-AIDS (English)
                        1-800-344-SIDA (Spanish)
                        1-800-AIDS-TTY (hearing-impaired)
gopher://cdcnac.aspensys.com:72/11/

National AIDS Information Clearinghouse
1-800-458-5231
Post Office Box 6003
Rockville, Maryland 20849

National Institute for Allergy and Infectious Disease
(AIDS Section)
9000 Rockville Pike
Bethesda, Maryland 29892
gopher://odie.niaid.nih.gov./11/aids/

National Institutes of Health: Safer Sex Documents
9000 Rockville Pike
Bethesda, Maryland 29892
gopher://gopher.niaid.nih.gov:70/11/aids/comm/teach

American Civil Liberties Unition (ACLU): HIV and AIDS
http://www.aclu.org/issues/aids/hmaids.html

LEGAL CONCERNS

Lesbian and Gay Lawnotes
http://www.qrd.org/qrd/www/usa/legal/lgln

Gay and Lesbian Alliance Against Defamation (GLAAD)
150 W. 26th Street, Suite 503
New York, New York 10001
http://www.glaad.org/glaad

National Gay and Lesbian Task Force (NGLTF)
2320 17th Street, NW
Washington, DC 20009
http://www.ngltf.org/ngltf

Human Rights Campaign Fund
1012 14th Street NW, Suite 607
Washington, DC 20005
http://www.hrcusa.org

Human Rights Campaign's National Coming Out Project
www.hrcusa.org/ncop/index.htm

Lambda Legal Defense and Education Fund
666 Broadway, Suite 1200
New York, New York 10012
http://qrd.tcp.com/qrd/orgs/LLDEF

American Association of Physicians for Human Rights
(Gay and Lesbian Medical Association)
1940 16th Street, No. 105
San Francisco, California 94103
http://www.glma.org

**American Civil Liberties Union (ACLU): Lesbian
and Gay Rights**
132 W. 43rd Street
New York, New York 10036
http://www.aclu.org/issues/gay/hmgl.html

Amnesty International: Lesbian and Gay Concerns
http://qrd.tcp.com/qrd/orgs/AIMLGC

International Gay and Lesbian Human Rights Commission
http://www.iglhrc.org/

RELIGIOUS ISSUES

Interfaith Working Group
Post Office Box 11706
Philadelphia, Pennsylvania 19101
http://www.libertynet.org:80/~iwg

World Congress of Gay and Lesbian Jewish Organizations
Post Office Box 18961
Washington, DC 20036

Gay Jews Mailing List
gopher://israel.nysernet.org:70/11/lists/gayjews

Dignity (Catholic)
1500 Massachusetts Avenue NW, Suite 11
Washington, DC 20005
http://www.dignityusa.org

Presbyterians for Lesbian and Gay Concerns
http://www.epp.cmu.edu/~riley/PLGC.html

Universal Fellowship of Metropolitan Community Churches
5300 Santa Monica Boulevard, No. 304
Los Angeles, California 90029
http://gpu.srv.ualberta.ca/~cbidwell/UFMCC/uf-home.htm

Affirmation (Mormon)
Post Office Box 46022
Los Angeles, California 90046

Affirmation (Methodist)
Post Office Box 1021
Evanston, Illinois 60204

Integrity (Episcopal)
Post Office Box 19561
Washington, DC 20036

National Gay Pentecostal Alliance
Post Office Box 1391
Schenectady, New York 12301

Gay Unitarians/Universalists: Office of Lesbian, Bisexual, and Gay Concerns
http://www.uua.org

Unitarian/Universalist Association
25 Beacon Street
Boston, Massachusetts 02108

Notes

Chapter 1

1. Hamer, Hu, Magnuson, Hu, and Pattatuci, 1993.
2. LeVay and Hamer, 1994.
3. Hamer, Hu, Magnuson, Hu, and Pattatuci, 1993.
4. In Dolce, 1993.
5. McCormick, Witelson, and Kingstone, 1990.
6. Dolce, 1993, p. 40.
7. Sanders and Ross-Field, 1986.
8. In Burr, 1993.
9. LeVay, 1993, p. 121.
10. LeVay and Hamer, 1994.
11. Allen and Gorski, 1991.
12. LeVay and Hamer, 1994.
13. Bull, 1993.
14. LeVay and Hamer, 1994, p. 49.
15. Green, 1987.
16. In LeVay, 1991.
17. In Isay, 1989.
18. Burr, 1993.
19. Louganis and Marcus, 1995, p. 74.
20. Borhek, 1993, p. 94.
21. Troiden, 1979, p. 363.
22. Ibid., p. 363.
23. Kooden, Riddle, Rogers, Sang, and Strassburger, 1979.
24. McDonald, 1982.
25. Anderson, 1987.
26. Troiden, 1979.
27. Ibid.
28. Hetrick and Martin, 1987, p. 39.
29. Ibid.
30. Rios, 1994.
31. Fisher, 1972, p. 249.
32. Gibson, 1994.
33. Heron, 1994, p. 139.
34. Masters and Johnson, 1979.
35. Dank, 1971.

36. Thielicke, 1964, p. 276.
37. Hetrick and Martin, 1987.
38. Ibid.
39. Heron, 1994, p. 119.
40. Dank, 1971.
41. McDonald, 1982.
42. Dank, 1971.
43. Troiden, 1979, p. 365.
44. McDonald, 1982.
45. Troiden, 1979, p. 368.
46. Dank, 1971.
47. McDonald, 1982.
48. Troiden, 1979.
49. Hetrick and Martin, 1987, p. 35.
50. Anderson, 1987.
51. Hetrick and Martin, 1987, p. 35.
52. Heron, 1994, pp. 119-120.
53. Ibid.
54. Pallone and Steinberg, 1990, p. 18.
55. Carrier, 1985.
56. Hetrick and Martin, 1987.
57. Troiden, 1979, p. 371.
58. Miller, 1979.
59. Coleman, 1982.
60. Troiden, 1979.

Chapter 2

1. *San Francisco Examiner*, 1989.
2. Robinson, Walters, and Skeen, 1989, p. 66.
3. Griffin, Wirth, and Wirth, 1986, p. 84.
4. Borhek, 1983.
5. Ibid., p. 20.
6. Weinberger and Millham, 1979.
7. Borhek, 1983.
8. Savin-Williams, 1989.
9. Robinson, Walters, and Skeen, 1989.
10. Ibid.
11. Weinberg, 1972, p. 97.
12. Robinson, Walters, and Skeen, 1989, pp. 66-67.
13. Barret and Robinson, 1990, p. 105.
14. Ibid.
15. Robinson, Walters, and Skeen, 1989, p. 66.
16. DeVine, 1984.
17. Hetrick and Martin, 1987.

18. Ibid.
19. Ibid., p. 35.
20. Bales, 1985.
21. Griffin, Wirth, and Wirth, 1986, pp. 10-11.
22. Weinberg, 1972.
23. DeVine, 1984.
24. Collins and Zimmerman, 1983.
25. Boswell, 1980.
26. In Buxton, 1991.
27. Gochros, 1985.
28. van der Geest, 1993.
29. Hatterer, 1974.
30. Strommen, 1989.
31. Ibid., p. 49.
32. Bozett, 1981.
33. Buxton, 1991.
34. Ibid., p. 11.
35. Bozett, 1981, pp. 554-555.
36. Coleman, 1985.
37. Strommen, 1989.
38. Harry, 1983.
39. Buxton, 1991.
40. Jones, 1978.
41. Dunne, 1987.
42. Bigner and Jacobsen, 1992, p. 109.
43. Miller, 1979.
44. Barret and Robinson, 1990.
45. Green, 1978.
46. Barret and Robinson, 1990.
47. Hitchens, 1980.
48. Golombek, Spencer, and Rutter, 1983.
49. Barret and Robinson, 1990.
50. Green, 1978.
51. Bozett, 1989.
52. Barret and Robinson, 1990.
53. Ibid., p. 77.
54. Savin-Williams, 1989.
55. Willhoite, 1991; Heron, Maran, and Kovick, 1994.

Chapter 3

1. *San Francisco Examiner*, 1989.
2. Harbeck, 1992b.
3. Griffin, 1992.
4. Harbeck, 1992a.

5. Griffin, 1992.
6. Dankmeijer, 1993.
7. Ibid., p. 100.
8. Harbeck, 1992b.
9. Ibid., p. 126.
10. Ibid., pp. 130-131.
11. Griffin, 1992.
12. Ibid., p. 191.
13. Williams, 1996, p. 83.
14. Ibid., p. 72.
15. Overlooked Opinions, 1992.
16. Friskopp and Silverstein, 1995.
17. Woods and Lucas, 1993.
18. Ibid., p. 186.
19. Schmitt and Kurdek, 1987.
20. PERSEREC/Sarbin and Karols, 1988.
21. PERSEREC/McDaniel, 1989, p. 21.
22. Clinton, 1993.
23. Shilts, 1993.
24. Zeeland, 1993, pp. 81-82.
25. Ibid., p. 99.

Chapter 4

1. Barbone and Rice, 1994, p. 104.
2. Bush, 1982.
3. Lewis, 1995, p. 75.
4. McCarthy, 1994, p. 39.
5. Mayo and Gunderson, 1994, p. 53.
6. Bauman, 1986.
7. Ibid., p. 75.
8. Shilts, 1987, p. 577.
9. Bush, 1983.
10. Kramer, 1989, p. 45.
11. Shilts, 1982, p. 362.
12. Ibid., p. 374.
13. Perry and Swicegood, 1991.
14. Rutledge, 1992.
15. Cammermeyer and Fisher, 1994, p. 296.
16. Ibid., p. 291.
17. Perry and Swicegood, 1991.
18. Ibid., p. 134.
19. Ibid., p.150.
20. Herek, Jobe, and Carney, 1996.
21. Ibid., pp. 213-214.

22. Ibid.
23. Perry and Swicegood, 1991.
24. Ibid.
25. Rasi and Rodriguez-Nogues, 1995.
26. Frank, 1997.

Bibliography

Chapter 1

Allen, L., and Gorski, R. (1991). Sexual dimorphism of the anterior commissure and massa intermedia of the human brain. *Journal of Comparative Neurology 12:* 97-104.

Anderson, D. (1987). Family and peer relations of gay adolescents. *Adolescent Psychiatry 14:* 162-178.

Borhek, M. (1993). *Coming out to parents: A two-way survival guide for lesbians and gay men and their families.* Cleveland, OH: The Pilgrim Press.

Bull, C. (August 24, 1993). Mom's fault? *The Advocate 636:* 30-32.

Burr, C. (March, 1993). Homosexuality and biology. *The Atlantic Monthly 271* (3): 47-65.

Carrier, J. (1985). Mexican male bisexuality. In F. Klein and T. Wolf (eds.), *Bisexualities: Theory and research.* Binghamton, NY: The Haworth Press.

Coleman, E. (1982). Developmental stages of the coming-out process. In *Homosexuality: Social, psychological and biological issues.* Society for the Psychological Study of Social Issues. Beverly Hills, CA: Sage Publications.

Dank, B. (1971). Coming out in the gay world. *Psychiatry 34:* 180-197.

Dolce, J. (June 1, 1993). And how big is yours? *The Advocate 630:* 38-44.

Fisher, P. (1972). *The gay mystique: The myth and reality of male homosexuality.* New York: Stein and Day.

Gibson, P. (1994). Gay male and lesbian youth suicide. In G. Remafedi (ed.), *Death by denial.* Los Angeles: Alyson Publications.

Green, R. (1987). *The "sissy boy" syndrome and the development of homosexuality.* New Haven, CT: Yale University Press.

Hamer, D., Hu, S., Magnuson, V., Hu, N., and Pattatuchi, M. (July 16, 1993). A linkage between DNA markers on the X chromosome and male sexual orientation. *Science 261:* 321-327.

Heron, A. (ed.) (1994). *Two teenagers in twenty: Writings by gay and lesbian youth.* Los Angeles: Alyson Publications.

Hetrick, E., and Martin, D. (1987). Developmental issues and their resolution for gay and lesbian adolescents. *Journal of Homosexuality 14:* 25-43.

Isay, R. (1989). *Being homosexual.* New York: Farrar, Straus and Giroux, Inc.

Kooden, H., Morin, S., Riddle, D., Rogers, M., Sang, B., and Strassburger, F. (September, 1979). Removing the stigma: Final report of the Board of Social and Ethical Responsibility for Psychology's Task Force on the Status of Lesbian and Gay Male Psychologists. Washington, DC: American Psychological Association.

LeVay, S. (1991). A difference in hypothalamic structure between heterosexual and homosexual men. *Science 253:* 1034-1037.

LeVay, S. (1993). *The sexual brain.* Cambridge, MA: The MIT Press [Bradford Books].

LeVay, S., and Hamer, D. (May, 1994). Evidence for a biological influence in male homosexuality. *Scientific American:* 44-49.

Louganis, G., and Marcus, E. (1995). *Breaking the surface.* New York: Random House.

Masters, W., and Johnson, V. (1979). *Homosexuality in perspective.* Boston: Little, Brown and Company.

McCormick, C., Witelson, S., and Kingston, E. (1990). Left-handedness in homosexual men and women: Neuroendocrine implications. *Psychoneuroendocrinology 15:* 69-76.

McDonald, G. (1982). Individual differences in the coming-out process for gay men: Implications for theoretical models. *Journal of Homosexuality 8* (1):47-60.

Miller, B. (1979). Unpromised paternity: Lifestyles of gay fathers. In M. Levine (ed.), *Gay men: The sociology of male homosexuality.* New York: Harper and Row.

Pallone, D., and Steinberg, A. (1990). *Behind the mask: My double life in baseball.* New York: Viking Press (Penguin Books).

Rios, D. (December 11, 1994). Being gay traumatic for teenagers. *The Times Picayune,* A-26.

Sanders, G., and Ross-Field, L. (1986). Sexual orientation and visuo-spatial ability. *Brain and Cognition 5:* 280-290.

Thielicke, H. (1964). *The ethics of sex.* New York: Harper and Row.

Troiden, R. (November, 1979). Becoming homosexual: A model of gay identity acquisition. *Psychiatry 42:* 362-373.

Chapter 2

Bales, J. (1985). Gay adolescents' pain compounded. *APA Monitor 16* (12): 21.

Barret, R., and Robinson, B. (1990). *Gay fathers.* San Francisco: Jossey-Bass (Lexington Books).

Bigner, J., and Jacobsen, R. (1992). Adult responses to child behavior and attitudes toward fathering: Gay and nongay fathers. *Journal of Homosexuality 23* (3): 99-112.

Borhek, M. (1983). *Coming out to parents: A two-way survival guide for lesbians and gay men and their parents.* New York: Pilgrim Press.

Boswell, J. (1980). *Christianity, social tolerance, and homosexuality: Gay people in Western Europe from the beginning of the Christian era to the fourteenth century.* Chicago: The University of Chicago Press.

Bozett, F. (July, 1981). Gay fathers: Evolution of the gay-father identity. *American Journal of Orthopsychiatry 51* (3): 552-559.

Bozett, F. (1989). Gay fathers: A review of the literature. *Journal of Homosexuality 18:* 137-162.

Buxton, A. (1991). *The other side of the closet: The coming-out crisis for straight spouses and families.* New York: John Wiley and Sons.

Coleman, E. (1985). Integration of male bisexuality and marriage. *Journal of Homosexuality 99* (1/2): 189-207.

Collins, L., and Zimmerman, N. (1983). Homosexual and bisexual issues. In J. Hansen, J. Woody, and R. Woody (eds.), *Sexual issues in family therapy.* Rockville, MD: Aspen Publications.

DeVine, J. (1984). A systemic inspection of affectional preference orientation and the family of origin. *Journal of Social Work and Human Sexuality 2:* 9-17.

Dunne, D. (1987). Helping gay fathers come out to their children. *Journal of Homosexuality 14* (1/2): 213-222.

Gochros, J. (1985). Wives' reactions to learning that their husbands are bisexual. *Journal of Homosexuality 11* (1/2): 101-113.

Golombok, S., Spencer, A., and Rutter, M. (1983). Children in lesbian and single-parent households: psychosexual and psychiatric appraisal. *Journal of Child Psychology, Psychiatry, and Allied Disciplines 24:* 551-572.

Green, R. (June, 1978). Sexual identity of 37 children raised by homosexual or transsexual parents. *American Journal of Psychiatry 135* (6): 692-697.

Griffin, C., Wirth, M., and Wirth, A. (1986). *Beyond acceptance: Parents of lesbians and gays talk about their experiences.* New York: St. Martin's Press.

Harry, J. (1983). Gay male and lesbian relationships. In E. Macklin and R. Rubin (eds.), *Contemporary families and alternative lifestyles.* Beverly Hills, CA: Sage Publications.

Hatterer, M. (March, 1974). The problems of women married to homosexual men. *American Journal of Psychiatry 131* (3): 275-277.

Hernon, A., Maran, M., and Kovick, K. (1994). *How would you feel if your dad was gay?* Los Angeles: Alyson Publications (Alyson Wonderland Division).

Hetrick, E., and Martin, A. (1987). Developmental issues and their resolution for gay and lesbian adolescents. *Journal of Homosexuality 14* (1/2): 25-43.

Hitchens, D. (1980). Social attitudes, legal standards, and personal trauma in child custody cases. *Journal of Homosexuality 5:* 89-95.

Jones, C. (1978). *Understanding gay relatives and friends.* New York: Seabury Press.

Miller, B. (1979). Unpromised paternity: The lifestyles of gay fathers. In M. Levine (ed.), *Gay men.* New York: Harper and Row.

Robinson, B., Walters, L., and Skeen, P. (1989). Responses of parents to learning that their child is homosexual and concern over AIDS: A national study. *Journal of Homosexuality 18* (1/2): 59-80.

San Francisco Examiner (June 6, 1989). Poll, p. 19.

Savin-Williams, R. (1989). Coming out to parents and self-esteem among gay and lesbian youths. *Journal of Homosexuality 18* (1/2): 1-35.

Strommen, E. (1989). "You're a what?" Family member reactions to the disclosure of homosexuality. *Journal of Homosexuality 18* (1/2): 37-58.

van der Geest, H. (1993). Homosexuality and marriage. *Journal of Homosexuality 23:* 115-123.

Weinberg, G. (1972). *Society and the healthy homosexual.* New York: St. Martin's Press.

Weinberger, L., and Millham, J. (1979). Attitudinal homophobia and support of traditional sex roles. *Journal of Homosexuality 4:* 237-246.

Willhoite, M. (1991). *Daddy's roommate.* Los Angeles: Alyson Publications (Alyson Wonderland Division).

Chapter 3

Clinton, W. (July 19, 1993). Proposed changes to current military policy (official address).

Dankmeijer, P. (1993). The construction of identities as a means of survival: Case of gay and lesbian teachers. *Journal of Homosexuality 24* (3/4): 95-105.

Friskopp, A., and Silverstein, S. (1995). *Straight jobs, gay lives: Gay and lesbian professionals, the Harvard Business School, and the American workplace.* New York: Scribner.

Griffin, P. (1992). From hiding out to coming out: Empowering lesbian and gay educators. *Journal of Homosexuality 22* (3): 167-196.

Harbeck, K. (1992a). Introduction (special issue: Coming out of the classroom closet.) *Journal of Homosexuality 22* (3): 1-7.

Harbeck, K. (1992b). Gay and lesbian educators: Past history/future prospects. *Journal of Homosexuality 22* (3): 121-140.

McDaniel, M. (January, 1989). *Preservice adjustment of homosexual and heterosexual military accessions: Implications for security clearance suitability.* PERS-TR-89-004. Monterey, California: Defense Personnel Security Research and Education Center. Reprinted in *Gays in Uniform: The Pentagon's Secret Reports*, K. Dyer (ed.). Boston: Alyson Publications.

Overlooked Opinions. (August, 1992). *In full view* (Newsletter/poll). Vol. 2 (1). Chicago: Author.

San Francisco Examiner. (June 6, 1989). Poll, p. 19.

Sarbin, T., and Karols, K. (December, 1988). *Nonconforming sexual orientations and military suitability.* PERS-TN-89-002. Monterey, California: Defense Personnel Security Research and Education Center. Reprinted in *Gays in Uniform: The Pentagon's Secret Reports*, K. Dyer (ed.). Boston: Alyson Publications.

Schmitt, P., and Kurdek, L. (1987). Personality correlates of positive identity and relationship involvement in gay men. *Journal of Homosexuality 13* (4): 101-109.

Shilts, R. (1993). *Conduct unbecoming: Lesbians and gays in the U.S. military, Vietnam to the Persian Gulf.* New York: St. Martin's Press.

Williams, W. (1996). Being gay and doing fieldwork. In E. Lewin and W. Leap (ed.), *Out in the field.* Chicago: University of Illinois Press, pp. 70-85.

Woods, J., and Lucas, J. (1993). *The corporate closet: The professional lives of gay men in America.* New York: The Free Press.

Zeeland, S. (1993). *Barrack buddies and soldier lovers: Dialogues with gay young men in the U. S. military.* Binghamton, NY: Harrington Park Press.

Chapter 4

Barbone, S., and Rice, L. (1994). Coming out, being out, and acts of virtue. *Journal of Homosexuality 27* (3/4). 91-110.

Bauman, R. (1986). *The gentleman from Maryland: The conscience of a gay conservative.* New York: Arbor House.

Bush, L. (April, 27, 1982). Naming gay names. *Village Voice.* Reprinted in L. Gross (ed.), *Contested closets: The politics and ethics of outing* (1993). Minneapolis: University of Minnesota Press.

Bush, L. (September 15, 1983). Gerry Studds. *The Advocate,* Issue 383, p. 15.

Cammermeyer, M., and Fisher, C. (1994). *Serving in silence.* New York: Penguin Books.

Frank, B. (January 28, 1997). Personal communication.

Herek, G., Jobe, J., and Carney, R. (1996). *Out in force: Sexual orientation and the military.* Chicago: University of Chicago Press.

Kramer, L. (1989). *Reports from the Holocaust: The making of an AIDS activist.* New York: St. Martin's Press.

Lewis, M. (1995). *Shame: The exposed self.* New York: The Free Press.

Mayo, D., and Gunderson, M. (1994). Privacy and the ethics of outing. *Journal of Homosexuality 27* (3/4): 47-65.

McCarthy, J. (1994). The closet and the ethics of outing. *Journal of Homosexuality 27* (3/4): 27-45.

Perry, T., and Swicegood, T. (1991). *Profiles in gay and lesbian courage.* New York: St. Martin's Press.

Rasi, R., and Rodriguez-Nogues, L. (1995). *Out in the workplace: The pleasures and perils of coming out on the job.* Los Angeles: Alyson Press.

Rutledge, L. (1992). *The gay decades: From Stonewall to the present—The people and events that shaped gay lives.* New York: Plume.

Shilts, R. (1982). *The mayor of Castro Street: The life and times of Harvey Milk.* New York: St. Martin's Press.

Shilts, R. (1987). *And the band played on: Politics, people, and the AIDS epidemic.* New York: St. Martin's Press.

Readers who wish to correspond with the author
should send their questions or concerns to:
MVargo@technologist.com
or to **merlin@comm.net**

Index

Order Your Own Copy of
This Important Book for Your Personal Library!

ACTS OF DISCLOSURE
The Coming-Out Process of Contemporary Gay Men

_____ in hardbound at $39.95 (ISBN: 0-7890-0236-1)

_____ in softbound at $17.95 (ISBN: 1-56023-912-3)

COST OF BOOKS_____

OUTSIDE USA/CANADA/
MEXICO: ADD 20%_____

POSTAGE & HANDLING_____
(US: $3.00 for first book & $1.25
for each additional book)
Outside US: $4.75 for first book
& $1.75 for each additional book)

SUBTOTAL_____

IN CANADA: ADD 7% GST_____

STATE TAX_____
(NY, OH & MN residents, please
add appropriate local sales tax)

FINAL TOTAL_____
(If paying in Canadian funds,
convert using the current
exchange rate. UNESCO
coupons welcome.)

☐ **BILL ME LATER:** ($5 service charge will be added)
(Bill-me option is good on US/Canada/Mexico orders only;
not good to jobbers, wholesalers, or subscription agencies.)

☐ Check here if billing address is different from
shipping address and attach purchase order and
billing address information.

Signature_____

☐ **PAYMENT ENCLOSED: $**_____

☐ **PLEASE CHARGE TO MY CREDIT CARD.**

☐ Visa   ☐ MasterCard   ☐ AmEx   ☐ Discover
☐ Diner's Club

Account #_____

Exp. Date_____

Signature_____

Prices in US dollars and subject to change without notice.

NAME_____

INSTITUTION_____

ADDRESS_____

CITY_____

STATE/ZIP_____

COUNTRY_____ COUNTY (NY residents only)_____

TEL_____ FAX_____

E-MAIL_____
May we use your e-mail address for confirmations and other types of information? ☐ Yes   ☐ No

Order From Your Local Bookstore or Directly From
The Haworth Press, Inc.
10 Alice Street, Binghamton, New York 13904-1580 • USA
TELEPHONE: 1-800-HAWORTH (1-800-429-6784) / Outside US/Canada: (607) 722-5857
FAX: 1-800-895-0582 / Outside US/Canada: (607) 772-6362
E-mail: getinfo@haworth.com
PLEASE PHOTOCOPY THIS FORM FOR YOUR PERSONAL USE.

BOF96